DATE DUE

PRINTED IN U.S.A.

GENETICALLY MODIFIED CROPS AND FOOD

EDITED BY NATALIE REGIS

Britannica®

Educational Publishing

IN ASSOCIATION WITH

ROSEN

EDUCATIONAL SERVICES

Published in 2016 by Britannica Educational Publishing (a trademark of Encyclopædia Britannica, Inc.) in association with The Rosen Publishing Group, Inc.
29 East 21st Street, New York, NY 10010

Distributed exclusively by Rosen Publishing.
To see additional Britannica Educational Publishing titles, go to rosenpublishing.com.

First Edition

Britannica Educational Publishing
J. E. Luebering: Director, Core Reference Group
Anthony L. Green: Editor, Compton's by Britannica

Rosen Publishing
Hope Lourie Killcoyne: Executive Editor
Natalie Regis: Editor
Nelson Sá: Art Director
Michael Moy: Designer
Cindy Reiman: Photography Manager
Introduction and supplementary material by Jeff Mapua.

Library of Congress Cataloging-in-Publication Data

Genetically modified crops and food / edited by Natalie Regis.—First edition.
    pages cm.—(The biotechnology revolution)
Audience: Grades 7 to 12
Includes bibliographical references and index.
ISBN 978-1-62275-578-3 (library bound)
1. Crops—Genetic engineering—Juvenile literature. 2. Transgenic plants—Juvenile literature.
3. Genetically modified foods—Juvenile literature. 4. Food—Biotechnology—Juvenile literature. I. Regis, Natalie, editor.
SB123.57.G477 2016
631.5'233—dc23

2014049175

Manufactured in the United States of America

Photo credits: Cover, p. 1 © iStockphoto.com/AndreasReh; pp. 6–7 Inga Spence/Science Source; pp. 20–21 Andre Held; p. 28 © Lisa Lubin/www.llworldtour.com; pp. 32–33 Science & Society Picture Library/Getty Images; pp. 37, 46, 72, 103, 126 Encyclopædia Britannica, Inc.; p. 38 Laguna Design/Science Source; pp. 48–49 © Elenathewise/Fotolia; p. 54 Archive Photos/Getty Images; p. 56 BSIP/Science Source; p. 60 Paolo Negri/Photographer's Choice RF/Getty Images; pp. 66–67 Nicholas J Reid/Photodisc/Getty Images; p. 79 Courtesy of the University of Guelph; pp. 80–81 Barcroft Media/Getty Images; p. 84 U.S. National Archives and Records Administration; pp. 90–91 Paul Grebilunas/The Image Bank/Getty Images; p. 93 Oliver Strewe/Lonely Planet Images/Getty Images; p. 100 CBS Photo Archive/Getty Images; pp. 106–107 Mark Bolton/Photolibrary/Getty Images; p. 115 Geri Lavrov/Moment Mobile/Getty Images; p. 119 AVTG/Vetta/Getty Images; p. 121 Michael Langford/Gallo Images/Getty Images; pp. 130–131 Danita Delimont/Gallo Images/Getty Images; p. 139 Sun Sentinel/McClatchy-Tribune/Getty Images; p. 150 Portland Press Herald/Getty Images; p. 153 Gail Jankus/Science Source/Getty Images; p. 156 Shulevskyy Volodymyr/Shutterstock.com; p. 164 Douglas Graham/CQ-Roll Call Group/Getty Images; cover and interior design elements vitstudio/Shutterstock.com (DNA), everythingpossible/iStock/Thinkstock (honeycomb), style_TTT/Shutterstock.com (linear patterns).

CONTENTS

CONTENTS

CONTENTS

INTRODUCTION

For some, the term "genetic modification" may conjure up images of mutations and monstrous creations haphazardly fused together like the creature in Mary Shelley's *Frankenstein*. Opponents of genetically modified (GM) food sometimes use the term "frankenfood" to describe products that are engineered in some way by science. For others, genetic modification is just another step in the kind of selective breeding that farmers have been doing for centuries. They also see it as the only way to feed an increasing world population. However, the debate over whether genetically modified crops should be used in food, or developed at all, has become a political fight that seems to pit scientists, big businesses, and government regulators against concerned citizens and some scientists and doctors who feel that the long-term effects of consuming these foods needs careful study.

A genetically modified organism, or GMO, is a plant or animal whose cells have been changed by adding genes from another species. A newer form of genetic modification is irradiating the animal or plant cells to produce a desired mutation. The purpose of changing an organism's cells is to make the organism more useful to people. For example, some genetically modified crops have been altered to produce more per season.

Genetically engineered wheat at UC Berkeley, Berkeley, California.

Altering plants and animals is not a modern practice. People have bred plants and animals in ways that enhance features that are beneficial while reducing characteristics of the organisms that are less desirable. Even the myriad dog breeds today are the result of artificially selecting specific animals for preferred traits. However, this type of breeding technique takes advantage of naturally occurring variations in animals and crops. GMOs, on the other hand, utilize advances in genetic engineering for precise control over what changes occur in an organism. Genes from one species can be introduced into a completely unrelated species to create organisms that grow precisely the way a scientist wants them to.

There are more than 40 types of genetically modified plants around the world, and only a few of these are grown for commercial purposes. The most common genetically modified plants are corn, canola, soybean, and cotton. There are also types of genetically modified papaya, chrysanthemums, poplars, and spruce. Tobacco, rice, cranberries, raspberries, and walnuts have been genetically modified but are not grown in the United States for human consumption. Soy oil and cornstarch are used in food manufacturing, while most of the other GM crops go to livestock producers as feed for their animals.

Genetically modified organisms have been a part of plant food production since the late 20th century. In the United States, genetically engineered animals have not been approved for sale for human consumption. However, limiting GMOs to plants has not reduced the controversy surrounding them. Some of the most recognizable brands in America are not immune to critics of GMOs.

REAL-WORLD CHANGES

In early 2014, the breakfast cereal Cheerios underwent a change to its ingredients. General Mills, the maker of Cheerios, quietly removed GMOs from the popular product. A cereal made by Post called Grape Nuts is also GMO-free. However, some consumers have complained that the newly GMO-free products are also now vitamin-free. Investigations into what vitamins have to do with GMO labeling have revealed that the growth, manufacturing, and handling restrictions that govern non-GMO products might not apply to vitamins. It was simply easier for these companies to remove the vitamins in order to make the products free of GMOs. Another large company, Target, said that its food brand, Simply Balanced, would be 100% GMO-free by the end of 2014.

Ben & Jerry's is a large ice cream company with creative and unique flavours. One of those flavours, Coffee Heath Bar Crunch, was among the company's best-sellers. A key ingredient of the flavour was Heath bars, a toffee candy made by the Hershey Company. Heath bars are made with genetically engineered ingredients. This put Ben & Jerry's in an uncomfortable position after it promised to remove all GMO ingredients from its ice cream. The company changed the formula, but unfortunately, there were complaints that the new, GMO-free version of the flavour, introduced in 2014, simply did not taste as good as the original.

The Ben & Jerry's company has a long history of vocally supporting causes they believe in. The owners have been staunchly against the use of GMOs in food. They helped raise money in support of a Vermont law that requires companies to label their products if it uses GMO ingredients.

However, while Ben & Jerry's openly fight GMOs, its parent company, Unilever, supports anti-labeling laws. Labeling laws would require companies that use GMOs in their products to state so clearly on the product packaging. Currently, Ben & Jerry's CEO Jostein Solheim says that there's an agreement between his company and Unilever that allows the ice cream maker to continue supporting causes independent of the parent company.

Current buying trends show that consumers are increasingly more interested in GMO-free products. Agribusiness and food producers have had to try to find a way to satisfy customers while maximizing profits, which is at odds with using GMOs in food because genetic modification in most cases has greatly improved profitability.

Companies are slowly devising strategies to deal with the GMO controversy. Many corporations are fighting state labeling laws that require them to give consumers more information about the ingredients in their products. However, some are following the leads of companies like Kellogg's. While fighting GMO labeling in each state, food producers are quietly introducing non-GMO products.

As some companies are discovering, ridding their products of GMOs is not always a simple task. For Ben & Jerry's, they were able to replace one type of toffee candy with another, non-GMO version. For those in the supply chain, they must ensure that GMO products are completely separate from GMO-free products. Crops have to be grown a certain distance away from genetically modified crops to avoid accidental cross-contamination. Equipment that handles the crops has to be thoroughly cleaned when switching between genetically modified products and their natural counterparts. This includes harvesting equipment, processing facilities, manufacturing facilities, transport receptacles, and shipping containers.

Consumers have complained that some companies are not moving away from GMOs fast enough. Kashi, a natural food brand owned by Kellogg's, has warned their customers via their website that switching over to non-GMO products will "take up to several months or years." Kashi will have to change contracts with growers, find suitable farmland to grow their crops, and adapt their recipes to avoid the complaints over flavour that Ben & Jerry's experienced with their adapted toffee flavour ice cream.

SOME PROBLEMS WITH GMOS

In 1999, a laboratory undertook a study looking into a genetically modified corn called Bt corn. This type of corn includes a gene from a type of bacterium that naturally produces a toxin that acts as a pesticide. "Bt" is shorthand for *Bacillus thuringiensis*, soil-inhibiting bacteria. The toxin is effective against certain types of caterpillars, including the European corn borer. But concerns over Bt corn were raised when studies showed that the toxin was also having a negative effect on the population of monarch butterflies, an insect not considered to be a pest.

For the next two years, teams of researchers studied this controversial type of corn. Researchers found that the Bt toxin was carried on the pollen in the air into areas that contained milkweed, the type of plant monarch butterfly larvae survive on. The toxin was found to kill off 19% of the monarch population, while the survivors did not grow to be as large and had a higher mortality rate than the control group. Critics claimed that the first study used unrealistic levels of pollen and that monarch butterflies would not be near the corn when it sheds pollen. They found the risk of Bt corn to monarch butterflies to be low. Eventually, the Food and Drug Administration allowed Bt corn usage.

Unfortunately for the makers of Bt corn, the controversy did not end there. A brand of Bt Corn called StarLink corn was not approved for human consumption. It was and is only approved for animal feed. However, it was found in taco shells at Taco Bell. Kraft, the distributor of the taco shells, recalled any of their products that could contain StarLink corn. Despite their efforts StarLink corn was found in many other food products even outside of the United States. After three years, the company that made StarLink corn had spent hundreds of millions of dollars tracking down the product and settling claims from corn growers. While the amount of contaminated product available to consumers was significantly less, they had not tracked down all of it.

BENEFITS

With so much in question over genetically modified foods and crops, why is it still being produced? There must be a tangible benefit to pursuing this type of agricultural science despite the fact that so many people find it unacceptable.

Crops, farm animals, and soil bacteria are among the organisms that are frequently genetically modified for use in food. Plants can be genetically engineered in such a way that they are more resistant to insects.

This reduces the costs and need for pesticides, which have their own risks. Agricultural products can also be modified to provide more nutrients, thus enhancing nutrient composition and food quality.

Genetically modified crops can mature faster and tolerate a variety of normally toxic chemicals such as aluminum or boron. They can also be made to survive frost, drought, or other adverse environmental events. With higher ability to overcome hardships, GMOs are options for farmers in areas that might not otherwise be suitable for agriculture.

Additionally, crops can be engineered to raise their overall output. Corn, cotton, and soy have been altered to produce 20 to 30 percent more per season. This leads to lower production costs for food and drugs. More yield means better food security. More people can benefit from these crops. GMOs can be a matter of life and death for some communities around the world where drought and famine have ravaged the population.

Although genetically modified animals have not been approved for human consumption, scientists have been working on animal modifications as well. Animals have been altered in ways to increase yield in milk production, for example, and make the animals less likely to contract diseases. Salmon have been modified to grow larger and mature faster. Genetically modified cattle show resistance to mad cow disease, a dangerous condition that affects both the animals and the people who consume it.

CRITICISMS

Concern over unknown factors such as the long-term effects on humans fuels much of the controversy over GMOs. Specifically, critics point out that altering the genes of food, crops, and animals can lead to unknown consequences. The new versions of crops have different metabolisms, growth rates, and responses to the environment. GM crops also affect the surrounding environment.

Plants engineered to resist herbicides, chemical substances that are toxic to plants and are used to destroy unwanted vegetation, have given rise to "super weeds." These weeds are more resistant to herbicides which leads to the use of more herbicides. Therefore the benefit of using fewer herbicides with GMOs is canceled out. Gene transfer of pesticide, herbicide, or antibiotic resistance can cause imbalances in the environment as plants that were of no danger to people can grow wild, helping spread disease to plants and animals. Additionally, antibiotic-resistant genes that are introduced into plants can eventually harm the helpful bacteria found in a healthy human stomach.

One of the biggest questions over GMOs is a simple one: are they safe to eat? Critics claim that engineering food on a genetic level could affect its nutritional value in a negative way, or create allergens and toxins that can be harmful to people. When StarLink corn was accidentally introduced to the public, people complained of adverse reactions after consuming products made with this variety of Bt corn. Because GMOs like StarLink are created by introducing a protein from a different plant to a cell, thereby creating a new protein, the potential for new allergic reactions in people is increased. The Centers for Disease Control (CDC) took samples and tested them for an allergic response to Cry9C, the protein used in StarLink corn, but the results were inconclusive.

However in 2013, several grocery stores vowed not to sell genetically engineered seafood at the same time that the FDA was considering approving AquAdvantage Salmon for human consumption. The fish is Atlantic salmon with genes of the Pacific salmon to stimulate faster growth, as well as genes of the ocean pout to allow for year-round growth. The grocery stores argued that more testing on the fish was warranted, and that they were concerned about the food being healthy and sustainable. In fact, one study done on the mingling of genetically-modified salmon and their natural counterparts in the wild revealed alarming results. The offspring of the modified fish and the non-GMO fish were incapable of natural growth and development. This difficulty spread throughout the population, showing that GMOs can eventually threaten both modified and unmodified members of the species. Another study that mated GMO salmon with wild trout had even more disastrous results.

The offspring grew faster and were thought to be a potential threat to the other fish in the area, as their large size and quick growth might deplete the supply of food for wild salmon.

ECONOMIC EFFECTS

GM foods and crops can also lead to unforeseen changes in the economy. Critics say that private companies who claim ownership of the GMOs they create will not share them at a reasonable cost to the public. This will hurt the economy, critics say, and small farmers who cannot afford the high prices will be driven out of business. The studies done on this topic, however, paint a different picture. An analysis of 15 studies reveals that two-thirds of the benefits of first-generation genetically modified crops are shared from larger companies down to smaller businesses. The analysis shows that one-third of the benefits are shared in the opposite direction. While this study shows that the criticism of GMOs harming the economy is untrue for the present, there are no guarantees of future effects. For example, one of the criticisms is that GM seeds may not be able to be harvested for the following year's crops, which forces farmers to constantly buy new seeds from manufacturers.

The debate over GMOs is far from over. Emotions can become intense when debates take place over the future of genetically modified food and crops. Both critics and supporters are susceptible to hyperbole and truth stretching. Both sides are prone to accuse any form of media of taking one side or another. The aim of this book is to be balanced without emphasizing one side over the other.

Science has introduced the world to an incredible breakthrough. Will genetically modified organisms solve many of the food related issues facing the world? Or, like Dr. Frankenstein, will these scientists regret the day they unleashed a monster on the population?

CHAPTER 1

AGRICULTURE FROM DOMESTICATION TO GENETICS

I t would be difficult to look at the effects of GM foods and crops without first understanding the history of agriculture which is, at its base, managing resources for the benefit of humankind. Agriculture has no single, simple origin. A wide variety of plants and animals have been independently domesticated at different times and in numerous places. The first agriculture appears to have developed at the closing of the last Pleistocene glacial period, or Ice Age (about 11,700 years ago). At that time temperatures warmed, glaciers melted, sea levels rose, and ecosystems throughout the world reorganized. The changes were more dramatic in temperate regions than in the tropics.

Plowing and sowing in Thebes. Painting from Tomb No. 1, Sennedjem, Thebes, Egypt.

THE DEVELOPMENT OF AGRICULTURE ACROSS THE GLOBE

Although global climate change played a role in the development of agriculture, it does not account for the complex and diverse cultural responses that ensued, the specific timing of the appearance

of agricultural communities in different regions, or the specific regional impact of climate change on local environments. By studying populations that did not develop intensive agriculture or certain cultigens, such as wheat and rice, archaeologists narrow the search for causes. For instance, Australian Aborigines and many of the Native American peoples of western North America developed complex methods to manage diverse sets of plants and animals, often including (but not limited to) cultivation. These practices may be representative of activities common in some parts of the world before 15,000 years ago.

Plant and animal management was and is a familiar concept within hunting and gathering cultures, but it took on new dimensions as natural selection and mutation produced phenotypes that were increasingly reliant upon people. Because some resource management practices, such as intensively tending nondomesticated nut-bearing trees, bridge the boundary between foraging and farming, archaeologists investigating agricultural origins generally frame their work in terms of a continuum of subsistence practices.

Notably, agriculture does not appear to have developed in particularly impoverished settings; domestication does not seem to have been a response to food scarcity or deprivation. In fact, quite the opposite appears to be the case. It was once thought that human population pressure was a significant factor in the process, but research indicated by the late 20th century that populations rose significantly only after people had established food production. Instead, it is thought that—at least initially—the new animals and plants that were developed through domestication may have helped to maintain ways of life that emphasized hunting and gathering by providing insurance in lean seasons. When considered in terms of food management, dogs may have been initially domesticated as hunting companions, while meat and milk could be obtained more reliably from herds of sheep, goats, reindeer, or cattle than from their wild counterparts or other game animals. Domestication made resource planning a more predictable exercise in regions that combined extreme seasonal variation and rich natural resource abundance.

MODIFICATIONS TO PLANTS AND ANIMALS IN EARLY AGRICULTURE

The domestication of plants and animals caused changes in their form; the presence or absence of such changes indicates whether a given organism was wild or a domesticate. On the basis of such evidence, one of the oldest transitions from hunting and gathering to agriculture has been identified as dating to between 14,500 and 12,000 BCE in Southwest Asia. It was experienced by groups known as Epipaleolithic peoples, who survived from the end of the Paleolithic Period into early postglacial times and used smaller stone tools (microblades) than their predecessors. The Natufians, an Epipaleolithic culture located in the Levant, possessed stone sickles and intensively collected many plants, such as wild barley (*Hordeum spontaneum*). In the eastern Fertile Crescent, Epipaleolithic people who had been dependent on hunting gazelles (*Gazella* species) and wild goats and sheep began to raise goats and sheep, but not gazelles, as livestock. By 12,000–11,000 BCE, and possibly earlier, domesticated forms of some plants had been developed in the region, and by 10,000 BCE domesticated animals were appearing. Elsewhere in the Old World the archaeological record for the earliest agriculture is not as well known at this time, but by 8,500–8,000 BCE millet (*Setaria italica* and *Panicum miliaceum*) and rice (*Oryza sativa*) were being domesticated in East Asia.

In the Americas, squash existed in domesticated form in southern Mexico and northern Peru by about 10,000–9,000 BCE. By 5,000–3,000 BCE the aboriginal peoples of eastern North America and what would become the southwestern United States were turning to agriculture. In sum, plant and animal domestication,

5

and therefore agriculture, were undertaken in a variety of places, each independent of the others.

The development of agriculture involves an intensification of the processes used to extract resources from the environment: more food, medicine, fibre, and other resources can be obtained from a given area of land by encouraging useful plant and animal species and discouraging others. As the productivity and predictability of local resources increased, the logistics of their procurement changed, particularly regarding the extent to which people were prepared to travel in order to take advantage of seasonally available items. Group composition eventually became more stable, mobility declined, and, as a consequence, populations increased. Different groups in different parts of the world effected change in their agriculture by making changes to their methods, by domesticating plants and animals for personal use (either as food, or as hunting companionship—e.g. dogs), by moving to different places in order to have access to different kinds of foods, and even by manipulating the ground that they lived on to better accommodate different types of crops.

AGRICULTURAL MODIFICATIONS BY EARLY FARMERS

Different parts of the world domesticated plants and animals in their own ways. What worked in Asia may not have worked in the Americas, so techniques and methods were different.

SOUTHWEST ASIA

Southwest Asia includes areas that border Africa and Europe, such as the Middle East and Turkey, and areas as far east as Afghanistan. Dating as far back as 23,000 BCE, a small group of Upper Paleolithic people in what is now Israel harvested grass seeds and other plant foods. Village farming spread across Southwest Asia around 10,000 BCE and settled farming cultures were widespread 1,000 years after.

One of the oldest domesticated grains that researchers have discovered comes from the area now known as Turkey. The grain, einkorn from Nevali Çori, dates back to about 10,500 BCE. Einkorn is an ancestor of domesticated wheat. However, rye found at another site in Syria that was radiocarbon-dated to 12,000 BCE may be domesticated. The rye was found at a site called Abū Hureyra. It is the largest known site from the era when domesticating plants and animals began. The inhabitants relied on and harvested wild einkorn, rye, lentils, and vetch, while also exploiting the gazelles.

Over time, the people of Abū Hureyra expanded the types of cultigens they grew. A cultigen is a plant that has been deliberately altered or selected by humans, and known only in cultivation, especially one with no known wild ancestor. In Abū Hureyra, the cultigens eventually included barley, two forms of domesticated wheat (emmer and einkorn), and legumes. Legumes were helpful for maintaining soil health and enriching the plant protein in diets. A form of crop rotation was also used, where different crops are grown on the same piece of land in different seasons. This helped maintain soil health and fertility.

The sudden onset of a cool period from c. 12,700 to 11,500 BCE reduced the number of available wild resources. As a result, the people of Abū Hureyra expanded agriculture, and evidence suggests the rest of the region did as well, though they might have done so for different reasons. There are signs that people throughout Southwest Asia were already growing a wide variety of plants in a number of different environments by this time.

The people in the region known today as Iran were relatively mobile. They hunted wild goats and sheep which moved across the land and harvested wild grasses as they followed the animals. Sheep and goats eventually replaced gazelles as the primary animal food of Southwest Asia. The earliest evidence for sheep and goat herding dates back to around 10,500 BCE. The practice was to eat the males of the species to maintain a healthy number of breeding females. The wild ancestors of cattle, aurochs, were hunted by about 10,000 BCE. Domesticated cattle were not prevalent until about 8,000 BCE in Anatolia, a region of Turkey, and the Mediterranean coast.

After 10,000 BCE, the agricultural system combined grain-based economies and livestock-based economies. During the earliest period of this combination economy, hoes or digging sticks were used to break ground. Livestock were used to plant seeds by walking over seeded areas. Food storage included pit silos and granaries. Crop irrigation was also used in drier areas.

THE AMERICAS

Indigenous peoples in the Americas created a variety of agricultural systems based on a range of environments. Agriculture arose independently in at least three regions: South America, Mesoamerica, and eastern North America. Crop use first appeared in Mexico and South America around 9,000 and 8,000 BCE. In North America, evidence for crop use begins between 5,000 and 4,000 BCE. While Old World settlements were established before agriculture, villages and towns in the Americas were built only after the development of most crops.

One common technique used was swidden production, also known as slash-and-burn agriculture. Nutrients are added to the soil by burning trees and shrubs, helping extend the usefulness of fields and gardens. When field fertility declined and firewood

Rice terraces in Sa Pa, Vietnam.

became scarce, settlements moved.

Swidden agriculture was less common in Mayan and Aztec societies. There, complex irrigation systems were used to support their dense populations and utilize the landscape. The Inca in Peru and residents of northern Mexico built terraced fields along sloped lands. Tools such as foot plows and hoes were used to prepare the land. Dung from llamas and alpacas were used as fertilizer. None of the animals in the Americas were the right size or temperament for herding, so indigenous peoples domesticated fewer animal species.

There was a wide variety crops native to the Americas and used for food production. These included potatoes, squash, avocados, beans, cacao, coca, peanuts, chili peppers, cotton, pineapples, quinoa, tomatoes, tobacco, and much more. The most widely used crop was corn, or maize. It was grown nearly everywhere there was food production.

EAST ASIA

Farming communities arose sometime before 8,000 BCE in China. However, it is not known how much earlier it may have developed. Agricultural communities began to prosper between 8,000 and 7,000 BCE. By the 4th century CE, cultivation was more intensive here than in Europe.

Some farms used dry field production which is farming without the use of irrigation. Other farms located along rivers, lakes, and marshes in the Yangtze River were dependent on the annual rise and fall of water levels. Paddy fields were invented which mimicked the natural wetland habitats ideal for rice.

Water buffalo, pigs, and chickens were domesticated. Crops in northern China included foxtail and broomcorn millets, hemp, and Chinese cabbage. Rice was the major crop in southern China. Rice and millet agriculture expanded to the Korean peninsula and into Japan. Other crops grown were soybeans, red beans, wild buckwheat, and barnyard millet.

When iron tools became available to Chinese peasants, China underwent a revolution in agricultural technology. A small iron plow from 475 to 221 BCE has been found, and cattle-drawn plows appear in the 1st century BCE. Innovations like the three-shared plow and harrow developed over time, and by 1300, Chinese agricultural engineering reached a high level.

THE INDIAN SUBCONTINENT

Research indicates two early stages of agricultural development in South Asia. During an earlier stage from 9,500 to 7,500 BCE in the most northwestern area, barley was the dominant crop along with some types of wheat: einkorn, emmer, durum, and bread wheat. There was both wild and domesticated barley in the region at this time. The second stage, dating to about 7,000 BCE has evidence of cotton crops. This was probably locally domesticated.

Agriculture was well established throughout most of the subcontinent by 6,000 to 5,000 BCE. Little evidence of farm tools has survived. However, it is likely that cereals could have been sown in the fall after the annual flooding of rivers had receded. Then they would be harvested in the spring. This practice continues today.

EUROPE

The oldest European agricultural sites are found along the Mediterranean coast. Agriculture was developed at Franchthi Cave in Greece, a site occupied for more than 15,000 years. Wild emmer, lentils and grass peas also grew in the area at this time. Sheep, goats, pigs, barley, lentils, and types of wheat became common around 9,000 BCE. Cattle were added by 8,000 BCE. At about the same time, crops and livestock were introduced to the Iberian Peninsula, the region that includes Spain and Portugal. By 7,000 BCE, domesticated food and village-based agricultural lifestyles were established on the coastal plains of Macedonia.

The Starčevo-Cris culture (c. 7,500 BCE) northwest of the Black Sea were the earliest known peoples to develop agriculture in that region. They grew wheat, oats, barley, peas, and broomcorn millet. The temperate regions of Europe led to a focus on cattle, pigs, einkorn, and legumes. If it was possible, residents would incorporate local wild stock into their domesticated herds of animals. This practice helped their animals become accustomed to the climate of the region.

Interactions between groups of hunters and gatherers and agricultural peoples who were migrating to the area help spread agriculture. The first culture to show evidence of agriculture was the Linearbandkeramik, or LBK. The culture spread

A diorama depicting medieval ploughing in the 14th century.

rapidly between 7,300 BCE and 6,900 BCE. By 6,000 BCE food production was under way in the British Isles. By 5,000 BCE, farming was common in Western Europe. New food ideas were incorporated across Europe. In areas such as Hungary and Switzerland, some form of agriculture was adopted while people still practiced hunting.

By the time Romans ruled the land, crop farming and animal domestication were established. Selectively breeding their animals was not common. Cattle, sheep, pigs, and goats were some of the domesticated species. Romans had a preference for very fat animals to help feed the people. Seasonal migration was normal.

The medieval period lasted from 600 to 1,600 CE. The first half saw agricultural advancements such as complex tools and different arrangements of land division. But by the end of the 13th century, war, famine, and the Black Death wiped out much of the advances. Land could not be cultivated due to lack of labor, and farm yields plummeted.

DOMESTICATION OF PLANTS

Domestic plants differ from their wild ancestors because they have been modified by human labor to meet specific human needs. Wild fruits, nuts, and berries were probably the first plant foods of ancient peoples. Later, humans learned to dig up roots and scrape or pound them to a paste for eating. In the process of domesticating plants, people selected those varieties of certain wild plant species that had desirable features — such as large kernels or fruits —

and cultivated them for human use. What follows is an explanation of the methods that marked the beginning of agriculture.

EARLY DOMESTICATION METHODS

By 3,000 BCE humans had domesticated every major food plant known today. Primitive peoples worked by trial and error, without the scientific knowledge of modern plant breeders. The plants being grown by 3,000 BCE must have taken at least 5,000 years, and probably more than 10,000 years, to domesticate.

To create a settled agriculture, the first farmers probably selected perennials for cultivation—plants that live for several years and produce flowers and seeds over many seasons. The farmers set pieces of the plant—roots, buds, leaves, underground stems— in the ground to produce more plants like the parent. This is called vegetative reproduction. Other plants, called annuals, are replanted each year, usually from seeds. Early farmers learned to save seeds from their best plants to sow for the next year's crop. By patient selection from one season to the next, the farmers gradually improved the species.

Through the ages, certain plants have been so changed by domestication that their wild forebears can no longer be identified. Such is the case with corn (maize). Cabbage, cauliflower, kohlrabi, broccoli, and brussels sprouts can all be traced back to a single wild variety of cabbage native to the eastern Mediterranean area. Many of the common vegetables of today, however, are unknown in the wild state.

ANCIENT METHODS OF AGRICULTURE

The only farm implements primitive peoples had were the digging stick and wooden hoe. Thus, many areas were difficult for them to cultivate. Wooded land, however, was easily cleared by girdling and killing the trees and then burning the fallen timber. Once such land was cleared, it was comparatively easy to plant in the deep, loamy soil.

As the soil was exhausted of its nutrients, the land was abandoned and new forest was cleared. This sort of shifting agriculture is still practiced in some tropical regions.

By about 200 BCE, farmers were using a fallow system of agriculture. Each year one third of the land was left fallow, or not planted. This fallow land would regain its fertility as it lay idle. The fallow system of agriculture was the beginning of the crop rotation system used today.

PLANT IMPROVEMENT, BREEDING, AND RESEARCH

People have been improving plants from ancient times by simple selection—saving seeds and vegetative parts of the best specimens for planting the next year. Scientific plant breeding did not begin until the discovery of the principles of heredity and genetics. The patterns of inheritance of plant traits were unknown until Gregor Mendel's work was presented in 1865, and his work has guided scientific plant breeders ever since.

GREGOR MENDEL AND EARLY WORK IN GENETICS

The use of genetics to develop new strains of plants and animals has brought major changes in agriculture since the 1920s. Genetics as the science dealing with the principles of heredity and variation in plants and animals was established only at the beginning of the 20th century. Its application to practical problems came later.

The modern science of genetics and its application to agriculture has a complicated background, built up from the work of many individuals. Nevertheless, Gregor Mendel, a monk in Brünn, Moravia (now Brno, Czech Republic), is generally credited with its founding.

Mendel studied mathematics (especially combinatorial mathematics which would prove to be helpful in his later work on genetics) and physics before he entered the Augustinian monastery in 1843. He continued his studies and from 1851 to 1853, he studied at the University of Vienna, again paying attention to physics and mathematics, but he also

Principle of Independent Assortment

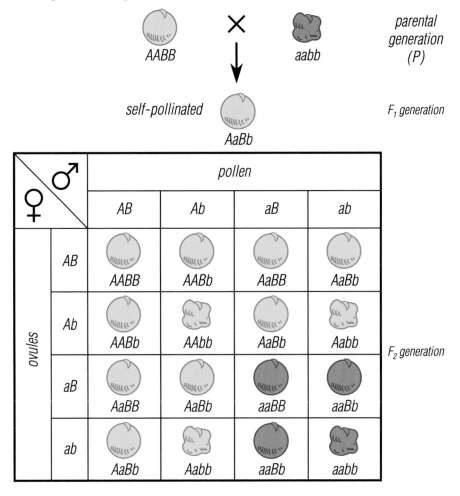

An illustration of Mendel's law of independent assortment. The example here shows a cross of peas having yellow and smooth seeds with peas having green and wrinkled seeds. A stands for the gene for yellow and a for the gene for green; B stands for the gene for smooth surface and b for the gene for a wrinkled surface.

added chemistry and plant physiology to his studies. On his return to the monastery, around 1854, Mendel

Mendel's First Law

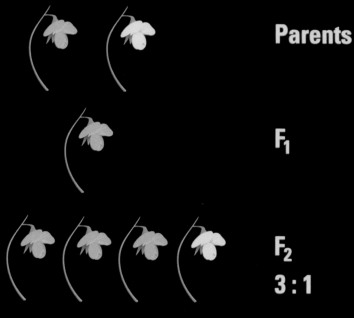

Parents

F_1

F_2
3 : 1

An illustration of Mendel's First Law, the genetic law of segregation. Violet and white flowers (Parents) produce a first generation with violet flowers (F1). The next generation gives a ratio of 3:1 violet to white flowers (F2).

was appointed to teach physics and natural history. The abbot also enlisted Mendel to undertake long-term research in hybridization. The abbot's aim was to increase the monastery's future profits from the wool of its Merino sheep. Mendel took on the project and focused not on animal hybridization, but on plants owing to the ease with which they could be manipulated. He intended to find out how hereditary characteristics were passed down through generations of hybrid progeny. The understanding up to that time was that the hereditary traits of the offspring of any species were an equal blending of the traits present in the parent species. It was also generally accepted that over many generations, a hybrid would revert to the original form. However, Mendel's research proved this was not the case. Plant and animal breeders had already shown that crossbreeding could produce new forms. Mendel's research showed that these hybrid forms were not produced by equally distributed traits from the parents, that they would not necessarily revert over several generations, and also that even hybrids could be used to create new forms.

To conduct his studies, Mendel chose the edible pea. Owing to the pea's many distinct varieties, and because progeny could be quickly and easily produced through successful seed germination and easy control of pollination, the pea proved an ideal research subject. From 1854 until 1856, Mendel tested 34 varieties of pea plants. He chose traits that were distinctive, such as plant height and seed color. Then he crossed varieties, mixing short with tall plants for example, or yellow-seed plants with green-seed plants. The resulting progeny displayed the character of one plant, but not the other, leading Mendel to theorize that some characteristics were dominant, and others recessive.

However, in subsequent hybrids, the recessive traits reappeared. In further testing, he identified that the characteristics selected in parent plants appeared in hybrid plants independently of each other. This has been called the law of independent assortment by the scientists who followed Mendel's work. Eventually, Mendel was able to predict the statistical likelihood of hybrid plants displaying one characteristic over another.

INTERPRETATION OF MENDEL'S WORK

What became known as the cell theory of fertilization came from Mendel's results that a new organism comes from the fusion of two cells. The law of segregation (another law that came from Mendel's work) shows that a hybrid had to be formed from cells that bore the potential to yield one characteristic or the other. Since one pollen cell fuses with one egg cell, all possible combinations of the differing pollen and egg cells would yield just the results suggested by Mendel's combinatorial theory.

Mendel first presented his results in two separate lectures in 1865 to the Natural Science Society in Brünn. His paper "Experiments on Plant Hybrids" was published the following year to little attention, although many libraries received it and reprints were sent out. Most readers overlooked the potential

REDISCOVERY OF MENDEL'S WORK

Mendel appears to have made no effort to publicize his work, and it is not known how many reprints of his paper he distributed. He had ordered 40 reprints, the whereabouts of only eight of which are known. Other than the journal that published his paper, 15 sources are known from the 19th century in which Mendel is mentioned in the context of plant hybridization. Few of these provide a clear picture of his achievement, and most are very brief.

Nearly 40 years after Mendel published his paper, Dutch botanist and geneticist Hugo de Vries, German botanist and geneticist Carl Erich Correns, and Austrian botanist Erich Tschermak von Seysenegg independently reported results of hybridization experiments similar to Mendel's. Though each later claimed not to have known of Mendel's work while doing their own experiments, both de Vries and Correns had read Mendel earlier. De Vries had a diversity of results in 1899, but it was not until he reread Mendel in 1900 that he was able to select and organize his data into a rational system. Of the three, Tschermak was the only one who had not read Mendel before obtaining his results, and his first account of his data offers an interpretation in terms of hereditary potency. However, in subsequent papers he incorporated the Mendelian theory of segregation and the purity of the germ cells into his text.

In Great Britain, biologist William Bateson became the leading proponent of Mendel's theory. Around him gathered an enthusiastic band of followers. However, Darwinian evolution was assumed to be based chiefly on the selection of small, blending variations, whereas

(*continued on the next page*)

(*continued from the previous page*)

Mendel worked with clearly nonblending variations. Bateson soon found that championing Mendel aroused opposition from Darwinians. He and his supporters were called Mendelians, and their work was considered irrelevant to evolution. It took some three decades before the Mendelian theory was sufficiently developed to find its rightful place in evolutionary theory.

The distinction between a characteristic and its determinant was not consistently made by Mendel or by his successors, the early Mendelians. In 1909 Danish botanist and geneticist Wilhelm Johannsen clarified this point and named the determinants genes. Four years later American zoologist and geneticist Thomas Hunt Morgan located the genes on the chromosomes, and the popular picture of them as beads on a string emerged. This discovery had implications for Mendel's claim of an independent transmission of traits, for genes close together on the same chromosome are not transmitted independently. Moreover, as genetic studies pushed the analysis down to smaller and smaller dimensions, the Mendelian gene appeared to fragment. Molecular genetics has thus challenged any attempts to achieve a unified conception of the gene as the elementary unit of heredity. Today the gene is defined in several ways, depending upon the nature of the investigation. Genetic material can be synthesized, manipulated, and hybridized with genetic material from other species, but to fully understand its functions in the whole organism, an understanding of Mendelian inheritance is necessary.

for variability and the evolutionary implications that his demonstration of the recombination of traits made possible. They tended to conclude that Mendel had demonstrated a widely-held belief that hybrid progeny revert to their originating forms. Most notably, Swiss botanist Karl Wilhelm von Nägeli actually corresponded with Mendel, despite remaining skeptical as to the significance of his results and doubting that the germ cells in hybrids could be pure.

Mendel's work went largely unknown until the early 20th century when other scientists began to experiment with botany and genetics. Once his work was rediscovered, he was generally accepted to be the father of genetics.

CHAPTER 2

GENETIC ENGINEERING AND CROP MODIFICATION

The application of genetics to agriculture has resulted in substantial increases in the production of many crops. This has been most notable in hybrid strains of maize and grain sorghum. At the same time, crossbreeding has resulted in much more productive strains of wheat and rice. Called artificial selection, or selective breeding, these techniques have become aspects of the larger and somewhat controversial field, genetic engineering. Of particular interest to plant breeders has been the development of techniques for deliberately altering the functions of genes by manipulating the recombination of DNA. This has made it possible for researchers to concentrate on creating plants that possess attributes — such as the ability to use free nitrogen or to resist diseases — that they did not have naturally.

SCIENTIFIC AGRICULTURE

Agricultural technology has developed more rapidly in the 20th century than in all previous history. Though the most important developments during the first half of the century took place in industrial countries, especially the United States, the picture changed somewhat after the 1950s. With the coming of independence, former colonies in Africa and Asia initiated large-scale efforts to improve their agriculture. In many cases they used considerable ingenuity in adapting Western methods to their own climates, soils, and crops. Scientific agriculture spurred on new methods in manipulating crops for better flavor, to eliminate problems with the end product, or to increase yield. In some cases, the method of planting or reaping the crop was changed, but in some cases the plant itself was modified.

While no truly new crop has been developed in modern times, new uses and new methods of cultivation of known plants may be regarded as new crops. For example, subsistence and special-use plants, such as the members of the genus Atriplex that are salt-tolerant, have the potential for being developed into new crops. New techniques, too, are the elaboration and systematization of practices from the past. The science of agriculture has developed to include genetic manipulation that changes plants not through domestication or hybridization, but through the manipulation of their genes.

27

GENETICS IN AGRICULTURE

The use of recombinant DNA (recombined genes from plants and microbes) in agriculture has allowed scientists to create crops that possess attributes that they did not have naturally and that improve crop yield or boost nutritional value. By manipulating plant genes, scientists have produced tomatoes with longer shelf lives and have produced pest-resistant potatoes. Genetic engineering has also been used to boost the nutritional value of some foods. "Golden rice" is a

Recombinant DNA is formed by using a restriction enzyme that cuts the double strand at a particular point. The same enzyme is used to cut a second piece of DNA. When the fragments are mixed together, the complementary ends of each strand will bind with those of the other, forming a recombinant DNA molecule.

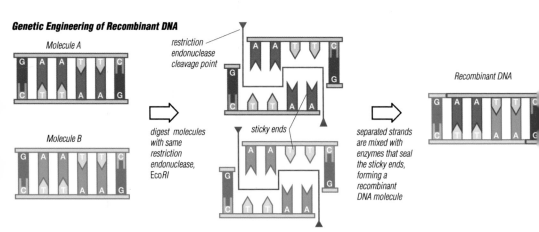

Genetic Engineering of Recombinant DNA

variety of white rice to which the gene for beta-carotene—a precursor of vitamin A—has been added. This nutrient-dense rice was developed for populations in less-developed countries where rice is a staple and where vitamin-A deficiency is widely prevalent.

The techniques of genetic engineering can be used to manipulate the genetic material of a cell in order to produce a new characteristic in an organism. Genes from plants, microbes, and animals can be recombined and introduced into the living cells of any of these organisms.

Organisms that have had genes from other species inserted into their genome (the full complement of an organism's genes) are called transgenic. The production of pathogen-resistant transgenic plants has been achieved by this method; certain genes are inserted into the plant's genome that confer resistance to such pathogens as viruses, fungi, and insects. Transgenic plants that are tolerant to herbicides and that show improvements in other qualities also have been developed.

Apprehension about the release of transgenic plants into the environment exists from consumers, ecologists and even some government agencies. Measures to safeguard the application of this technology have been adopted. In the United States several federal agencies, such as the U.S. Department of Agriculture, the Food and Drug Administration, and the Environmental Protection Agency, regulate the use of genetically engineered organisms. As of 2006, more than 250 million acres (100 million hectares) worldwide were planted with GM crops. Among the most successful GM crops are corn (maize), soybeans, and cotton, all of which have proved valuable to farmers with respect to producing increased yields and having economic advantages. In fact, the vast majority of the soybeans, cotton, and corn raised commercially in the United States are genetically modified. While many of the objections that have been raised have merit, it is unlikely that the use of genetic engineering in agriculture will be halted.

MODERN BREEDING METHODS

Scientific plant breeding uses three processes: hybridization, selection, and mutagenesis and genetic engineering.

Hybridization, as discussed previously in the work of Gregor Mendel, involves controlled crosses between two parent plants. The plant produced by a cross between varieties of the same species is known as a crossbreed. A plant produced by a cross between two different species is a hybrid. Pollen from the stamen, or male element, of one plant is transferred to the pistil, or female element, of another plant. The plant breeders hope that some of the seed that develops from this cross will inherit the new quality for which they are looking. If it does, they then try to "fix" that quality, or make it permanent, by inbreeding plants grown from the new seed for several generations. This means that the blossoms of the new plants are fertilized with their own pollen. From each successive generation of plants so produced, the breeders select as parents of the next generation those that have kept most successfully the qualities they desire. When the plant is finally "breeding true" with the qualities the breeder seeks, its seed is tested under varying conditions of soil and climate.

Triticale, a hybrid of rye and wheat.

Plant breeders may also use methods of cutting and grafting, especially when they are improving vines and fruit trees. The purpose of vegetative reproduction, however, is propagation of a desired plant, not the development of new varieties.

Mutations, also called breaks, are new characteristics that suddenly appear in a plant. They are not inherited from the parent plants but are caused by a spontaneous change in the plant cells' genes. Plant breeders are always watching for desirable mutations that can be developed into new varieties of plants. Mutations occur in nature only by chance. However, breeders can induce mutations by several means. The chemical colchicine causes doubling of chromosomes, the carriers of genes. Plants modified in this way are often more robust and bear larger flowers. Plant breeders have also used X-ray bombardment and irradiation from atomic reactors to cause mutations. They then select from among the mutant plants those that possess desirable traits.

The process of genetic engineering has provided new opportunities to plant breeders. By injecting the genes from one plant into the cells of another plant, scientists have produced new varieties of crop plants with desired traits.

Another approach to plant improvement is through the use of hormones, called growth regulators. For example, the hormone gibberellin is sometimes used to stimulate seed germination

BREEDING ACCOMPLISHMENTS

Hybrid corn represents one of the greatest accomplishments of plant breeding. Such hybrid varieties not only have greater food potential, but some also have enhanced industrial uses. For example, one variety of corn produces a form of starch that is used in the manufacture of paper, films, and fibers. Many other major crops, including soybeans and wheat, have benefited from plant breeding. Plant breeders have increased the sugar content of sugar beets from 7 to 25 percent. Similarly, the yield of dry sugar per acre of sugarcane has been increased more than 1,000 percent since 1844. New cotton varieties have stronger fibers than the old varieties. In addition, certain diseases of plants—wilt in alfalfa, rust in timothy, and many others—have been overcome by breeding resistant plant varieties.

In 1930 another accomplishment in breeding was achieved— this time, a legal one. The United States government recognized the breeders of new plants as inventors and passed a law allowing them to patent their products. In 1931 an everblooming rose named New Dawn became the first patented plant.

and to increase plant size. Chemicals called auxins are used to improve fruit quality. Although growth regulators improve the plants to which they are applied, the improvements are not inherited by the plants' offspring.

THE SCIENCE OF GENETICS

At the time that Gregor Mendel's work was rediscovered, the science of genetics was in its first stages of development. By 1903 scientists in the United States and Germany had concluded that genes are carried in the chromosomes, nuclear structures visible under the microscope. In 1911 a theory that the genes are arranged in a linear file on the chromosomes and that changes in this conformation are reflected in changes in heredity was announced.

Genes are highly stable. During the processes of sexual reproduction, however, means are present for assortment, segregation, and recombination of genetic factors. Thus, tremendous genetic variability is provided within a species. This variability makes possible the changes that can be brought about within a species to adapt it to specific uses. Occasional mutations of genes also contribute to variability.

Development of new strains of plants and animals did not, of course, await the science of genetics, and some advances were made by empirical methods even after the application of genetic science to agriculture. The U.S. plant breeder Luther Burbank, without any formal knowledge of genetic principles, developed the Burbank potato as early as 1873 and continued his plant-breeding research, which produced numerous new varieties of fruits and vegetables. In some instances, both practical experience and scientific knowledge contributed to major technological achievements.

THE MOST SUCCESSFULLY MODIFIED PLANTS

For the purposes of food production, some plant modifications have been more successful than others. Corn, for instance, has banked on the collective information from farmers' longtime experience with the plant as well as technological advances. Other plants that have also successfully benefitted from both experience and technology are wheat and rice. All three are staple foods across the globe.

MAIZE, OR CORN

Maize originated in the Americas, having been first developed by Indians in the highlands of Mexico. It was quickly adopted by the European settlers, Spanish, English, and French. The first English settlers found the northern Indians growing a hard-kernelled, early-maturing flint variety that kept well, though its yield was low. Indians in the south-central area of English settlement grew a soft-kernelled, high-yielding, late-maturing dent corn. There were doubtless many haphazard crosses of the two varieties. In 1812, however, John Lorain, a farmer living near Philipsburg, Pennsylvania, consciously mixed the two

LUTHER BURBANK

Luther Burbank

Luther Burbank, born March 7, 1849, Lancaster, Massachusetts, U.S.– died April 11, 1926, Santa Rosa, California, was an American plant breeder whose prodigious production of useful varieties of fruits, flowers, vegetables, and grasses encouraged the development of plant breeding into a modern science.

Reared on a farm, Burbank received little more than a high school education, but he was profoundly influenced by the books of Charles Darwin, especially *"The Variation of Animals and Plants Under Domestication"* (1868). At the age of 21 he purchased a 7-hectare (17-acre) tract near Lunenberg, Massachusetts, and began a

55-year plant-breeding career that almost immediately saw the development of the Burbank, or Idaho, potato. Selling the rights to the potato for $150 to use as travel fare to California, he settled in Santa Rosa, where he established a nursery garden, a greenhouse, and experimental farms that were to become famous throughout the world.

Burbank's breeding methods effected multiple crosses of foreign and native strains and produced seedlings that were grafted onto fully developed plants for a relatively quick appraisal of hybrid characteristics. At all stages of the process, he demonstrated an ability for extremely keen observation and the immediate recognition of desirable characteristics, which enabled him to select useful varieties. Indeed, he took the apparent "molding effect" he exercised on his plants as evidence for the inheritance of acquired characteristics, despite the publication of Gregor Mendel's principles of heredity in 1901 and the subsequent creation of the science of genetics.

Burbank developed more than 800 new strains and varieties of plants, including 113 varieties of plums, 20 of which are still commercially important, especially in California and South Africa; 10 commercial varieties of berries; and more than 50 varieties of lilies.

and demonstrated that certain mixtures would result in a yield much greater than that of the flint, yet with many of the flint's desirable qualities. Other farmers and breeders followed Lorain's example, some aware

Genetically modified corn.

of his pioneer work, some not. The most widely grown variety of the Corn Belt for many years was Reid's Yellow Dent, which originated from a fortuitous mixture of a dent and a flint variety.

At the same time, other scientists besides Mendel were conducting experiments and developing theories that were to lead directly to hybrid maize. In 1876 Charles Darwin published the results of experiments on cross- and self-fertilization in plants. Carrying out his work in a small greenhouse in his native England, the man who is best known for his theory of evolution found that inbreeding usually reduced plant vigor and that crossbreeding restored it.

Darwin's work was studied by a young American botanist, William James Beal, who probably made the first controlled crosses between varieties of maize for the sole purpose of increasing yields through hybrid vigor. Beal worked successfully without knowledge of the genetic principle involved. In 1908 George Harrison Shull concluded that self-fertilization tended to separate and purify strains while weakening the plants but that vigor could be restored by crossbreeding the inbred strains. Another scientist found that inbreeding could increase the protein content of maize, but with a marked decline in yield. With knowledge of inbreeding and hybridization at hand, scientists had yet to develop a technique whereby hybrid maize with the desired characteristics of the inbred lines and hybrid vigor could be combined in a practical manner. In 1917 Donald F. Jones of the Connecticut Agricultural Experiment Station discovered the answer, the "double cross."

The double cross was the basic technique used in developing modern hybrid maize and has been used by commercial firms since. Jones's invention was to use four inbred lines instead of two in crossing. Simply, inbred lines A and B made one cross, lines C and D another. Then AB and CD were crossed, and a double-cross hybrid, ABCD, was the result. This hybrid became the seed that changed much of American agriculture. Each inbred line was constant both for certain desirable and for certain undesirable traits, but the practical breeder could balance his four or more inbred lines in such a way that the desirable traits outweighed the undesirable. Foundation inbred lines were developed to meet the needs of varying climates, growing seasons, soils, and other factors. The large hybrid seed-corn companies undertook complex applied-research programs, while state experiment stations and the U.S. Department of Agriculture tended to concentrate on basic research.

The first hybrid maize involving inbred lines to be produced commercially was sold by the Connecticut Agricultural Experiment Station in 1921. The second was developed by Henry A. Wallace, a future secretary of agriculture and vice president of the United States. He sold a small quantity in 1924 and, in 1926, organized the first seed company devoted to the commercial production of hybrid maize.

Many Midwestern farmers began growing hybrid maize in the late 1920s and 1930s, but it did not dominate corn production until World War II. In 1933, 1 percent of the total maize acreage was planted with hybrid seed. By 1939 the figure was 15 percent, and in 1946 it rose to 69. The percentage was 96 in 1960. The average per acre yield of maize rose from 23 bushels (2,000 litres per hectare) in 1933, to 83 bushels (7,220 litres per hectare) by 1980.

The techniques used in breeding hybrid maize have been successfully applied to grain sorghum and several other crops. New strains of most major crops are developed through plant introductions, crossbreeding, and selection, however, because hybridization in the sense used with maize and grain sorghums has not been successful with several other crops.

WHEAT

Advances in wheat production during the 20th century included improvements through the introduction of new varieties and strains; careful selection by farmers and seedsmen, as well as by scientists; and crossbreeding to combine desirable characteristics. The adaptability of wheat enables it to be grown in almost every country of the world. In most of the

Three different types of wheat plants.

developed countries producing wheat, endeavors of both government and wheat growers have been directed toward scientific wheat breeding.

The development of the world-famous Marquis wheat in Canada, released to farmers in 1900, came about through sustained scientific effort. Sir Charles Saunders, its discoverer, followed five principles of plant breeding: (1) the use of plant introductions; (2) a planned crossbreeding program; (3) the rigid selection of material; (4) evaluation of all characteristics in replicated trials; and (5) testing varieties for local use. Marquis was the result of crossing a wheat long grown in Canada with a variety introduced from India. For 50 years, Marquis and varieties crossbred from Marquis dominated hard red spring wheat growing in the high plains of Canada and the United States and were used in other parts of the world.

In the late 1940s a short-stemmed wheat was introduced from Japan into a more favourable wheat-growing region of the U.S. Pacific Northwest. The potential advantage of the short, heavy-stemmed plant was that it could carry a heavy head of grain, generated by the use of fertilizer, without falling over or "lodging" (being knocked down). Early work with the variety was unsuccessful; it was not adaptable directly into U.S. fields. Finally, by crossing the Japanese wheat with acceptable varieties in the Palouse Valley in Washington, there resulted the first true semidwarf wheat in the United States to be commercially grown under irrigation and heavy applications of fertilizer. This first variety, Gaines, was introduced in 1962, followed by Nugaines in 1966. The varieties now grown in the United States commonly produce 100 bushels per acre (8,700 litres per hectare), and world records of more than 200 bushels per acre have been established.

The Rockefeller Foundation in 1943 entered into a cooperative agricultural research program with the government of Mexico, where wheat yields were well below the world average. By 1956 per acre yield had doubled, mainly because of newly developed varieties sown in the fall instead of spring and the use of fertilizers and irrigation. The short-stemmed varieties developed in the Pacific Northwest from the Japanese strains were then crossed with various Mexican and Colombian wheats. By 1965 the new Mexican wheats were established, and they gained an international reputation.

RICE

The success of the wheat program led the Rockefeller and Ford Foundations in 1962 to establish the International Rice Research Institute at Los Baños in the Philippines. A research team assembled some 10,000 strains of rice from all parts of the world and began outbreeding. Success came early with the combination of a tall, vigorous variety from Indonesia and a dwarf rice from Taiwan. The strain IR-8 has proved capable of doubling the yield obtained from most local rices in Asia.

Because of ongoing famine in certain parts of the world, rice, which was the staple food in many less-developed countries, was the focus of genetic research to increase its nutritional value. As previously mentioned, some researchers were working with "golden rice," a strain developed to contain beta-carotene, which the human body converts into vitamin A. In 2005 a new strain of "golden rice" that contained much higher levels of beta-carotene than earlier strains was announced, and its use was seen as a potential way of overcoming vitamin-A deficiency in the diets of many children in less-developed countries. In a breakthrough that was expected to speed the development of new strains of rice, geneticists in 2005 published the complete mapping of the genetic sequence of the rice genome.

CHAPTER 3

ANIMAL PRODUCE, FROM BREEDING TO BIOENGINEERING

As with crops, early farmers developed breeding as the controlled propagation of domestic animals in order to improve desirable qualities. Humanity has been modifying domesticated animals to better suit human needs for centuries. Selective breeding involves using knowledge from several branches of science. These include genetics, statistics, reproductive physiology, computer science, and molecular genetics. This chapter discusses the basic principles of how populations of animals can be altered by selective breeding, and will examine the controversy surrounding the creation and use of bioengineered animals.

BREEDING AND VARIATION

In animal breeding, a population is a group of interbreeding individuals — i.e., a breed or strain within a breed that is different in some aspects from other breeds or strains. Typically, certain animals within a breed are designated as purebred. The essential difference between purebred and non-purebred animals is that the genealogy of purebred animals has been carefully recorded, usually in a herd book, or studbook, kept by some sanctioning association. Purebred associations provide other services that are useful to their members to enhance their businesses.

Selective breeding utilizes the natural variations in traits that exist among members of any population. Breeding progress requires understanding the two sources of variation: genetics and environment. For some traits there is an interaction of genetics and the environment. Differences in the animals' environment, such as amount of feed, care, and even the weather, may have an impact on their growth, reproduction, and productivity. Such variations in performance because of the environment are not transmitted to the next generation. For most traits measured in domestic animals, the environment has a larger impact on variation than do genetic differences. For example, only about 30 percent of the variation in milk production in dairy cattle can be attributed to genetic effects; the

An organically raised Angus Bull.

remainder of the variation is due to environmental effects. Thus, environmental factors must be considered and controlled in selecting breeding stock.

Genetic variation is necessary in order to make progress in breeding successive generations. Each gene, which is the basic unit of heredity, occupies a specific location, or locus, on a chromosome. Two or more genes may be associated with a specific locus and therefore with a specific trait. (Traits that can be observed directly, such as size, color, shape, and so forth, make up an organism's phenotype.) These genes are known as alleles. If paired alleles are the same, the organism is called homozygous for that trait; if they are different, the organism is heterozygous. Typically, one of the alleles will be expressed to the exclusion of the other allele, in which case the two alleles are referred to as dominant and recessive, respectively. However, sometimes neither dominates, in which case the two alleles are called codominant.

BREEDING OBJECTIVES

Breeding objectives can be discussed in terms of changing the genetic makeup of a population of animals, where population is defined as a recognized breed. Choice of breeding goals and design of an effective breeding program is usually not an easy task. Complicating the implementation of a breeding program is the number of generations needed to reach the initial goals. Ultimately, breeding goals are dictated by market demand; however, it is not easy to predict what consumers will want several years in advance. Sometimes the marketplace demands a different product than was defined as desirable in the original breeding objective. When this happens, breeders have to adjust their program, which results in less-efficient selection than if the new breeding goal had been used from the beginning. For example, consumers want leaner beef that is tender. Thus, ranchers have changed their cattle-breeding programs to meet this new demand. These trends have gradually changed over the last few decades; for example, Angus cattle are particularly noted for the quality of beef produced. The use of ultrasound is now widespread in determining the fat and lean content of live animals, which will hasten the changing of carcass quality to meet consumer demands.

Additional complications arise from simultaneously trying to improve multiple traits and the difficulty of determining what part of the variation for each trait is under genetic control. In addition, some traits are genetically correlated, and this correlation may be positive or negative; that is, the traits may be complementary or antagonistic. Breeding methods depend on heritability and genetic correlations for desirable traits.

HERITABILITY AND GENETIC CORRELATIONS IN BREEDING

Heritability is the proportion of the additive genetic variation to the total variation. Heritability is important because without genetic variation there can be no genetic change in the population. Alternatively, if heritability is high, genetic change can be quite rapid, and simple means of selection are all that is needed. Using an increasing scale from o to

1, a heritability of 0.75 means that 75 percent of the total variance in a trait is controlled by additive gene action. With heritabilities this high, just the record of a single individual's traits can easily be used to create an effective breeding program.

Some general statements can be made about heritability, keeping in mind that exceptions exist. Traits related to fertility have low heritabilities. Examples include the average number of times that a cow must be bred before she conceives and the average number of pigs in a litter. Traits related to production have intermediate heritabilities. Examples include the amount of milk a cow produces, the rates of weight gain in steers and pigs, and the number of eggs laid by chickens. So-called quality traits tend to have higher heritabilities. Examples include the amount of fat a pig has over its back and the amount of protein in a cow's milk. The magnitude of heritability is one of the primary considerations in designing breeding programs.

Genetic correlation occurs when a single gene affects two traits. There may be many such genes that affect two or more traits. Genetic correlations can be positive or negative, which is indicated by assigning a number in the range from +1 to -1, with 0 indicating no genetic correlation. A correlation of +1 means that the traits always occur together, while a correlation of -1 means that having either trait always excludes having the other trait. Thus, the greater the displacement of the value from 0, the greater the correlation (positive or negative) between traits. The practical breeding consequence is that selection for one trait will pull along any positively correlated traits, even though there is no deliberate selection for them. For example, selecting for increased milk production also increases protein production. Another example is the selection for increased weight gain in broiler chickens, which also increases the fat content of the birds.

When traits have a negative genetic correlation, it is difficult to select simultaneously for both traits. For example, as milk production is increased in dairy cows through genetic selection, it is slightly more difficult for the high-producing cows to conceive. This negative correlation is partly due to the partitioning of the cows' nutrients between production and reproduction, with production being prioritized in early lactation. In the case of dairy cattle, milk production is on the order of 20,000 pounds (9,071 kilograms) per year and is increasing. This is a large metabolic demand, so nutrient demand is large to meet this need. Thus, selecting for improved fertility may result in a reduction in milk production or its rate of gain.

SELECTION

Types of selection are individual or mass selection, within and between family selection, sibling selection, and progeny testing, with many variations. Within family selection uses the best individual from each family for breeding. Between family selection uses the whole family for selection. Mass selection uses records of only the candidates for selection. Mass selection is most effective when heritability is high and the trait is expressed early in life, in which case all that is required is observation and selection based on phenotypes. When mass selection is not appropriate, other methods of selection, which make use of relatives or progeny, can be used singularly or in combination. Modern technologies allow use of all these types of selection at the same time, which results in greater accuracy.

THE GENETIC CODE (DNA) AND IMMUNOGENETICS

Traditional breeding systems can be an inexact science. Traits can be bred out of a species while others can be enhanced, but overall effectiveness is limited when compared to immunogenetics and DNA manipulation. The latter techniques are powerful tools that can permanently affect plants, animals, and what people eat in the future.

DNA

DNA is the genetic material that contains the instructions in each cell of organisms. DNA determines the genome, and thus the genetic code, which is a blueprint for development of all body organs and structures. The structure of DNA can be visualized as a spiral staircase. The handrails are made up of sugar and phosphate molecules, and the steps

DNA structure.

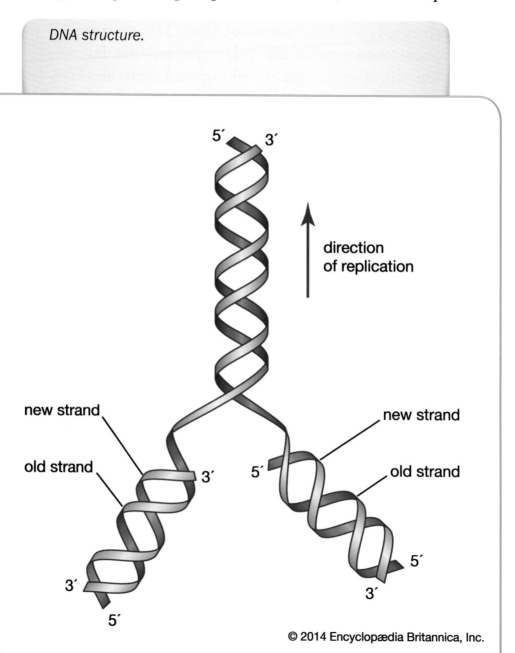

direction of replication

new strand

old strand

new strand

old strand

are composed of four nitrogenous bases: adenine (A), thymine (T), cytosine (C), and guanine (G). These bases are paired: adenine is paired with thymine, and cytosine is paired with guanine. The order of these four base pairs is the genetic code that determines the genotype of an individual. The DNA is arranged on chromosomes inside cells, with cells having two methods of dividing and replicating. In mitosis, a cell divides into two daughter cells such that each contains an exact copy of the original cell's chromosomes. In meiosis, a germ cell's chromosomes are duplicated before the cell undergoes two divisions to produce four gametes, or sex cells, each with half (male or female) of the original cell's chromosomes. During the process of fertilization, male and female gametes from different organisms pair their chromosomes to form a zygote, which eventually becomes an adult.

Genetic progress in domestic animals has been made using quantitative methods to date. It would be very desirable to know the genes that control the many traits that have economic significance in domestic animals. This should make selection more accurate. Information from sequencing human genes, as well as those of other species, is being used to find chromosomal segments with high probabilities of coding genes in livestock. Another approach is to scan a chromosome segment and look for associations with economic traits. Several quantitative trait loci have been discovered that are or promise to be useful in livestock breeding. For example, an estrogen receptor in pigs is associated with increased litter size—on average, an increase of 0.6 to 2.0 pigs per litter, depending on the genetic background in which the gene is expressed. Other genes have been found that control the secretion of casein in cow's milk. Genes are also known for growth hormone, and many others could be enumerated. With improvements in sequencing DNA, more genes will be discovered that affect economic traits—genes that will need to be tested in different genetic backgrounds and environments before they can be commercialized.

It is now much less expensive to sequence DNA, which has led to new methods of evaluating animals using large segments of 30,000–50,000 bases. With the use of these large segments of DNA, animals are evaluated without looking for markers for individual traits. This is intuitively an appealing approach because much more of the DNA can be evaluated; perhaps in the future the entire genome can be used to evaluate animals. This method of selection, called genomic selection, is now being applied to dairy cattle, but results are not yet available.

IMMUNOGENETICS

The connection between an organism's genetic makeup and its immune system, as well as applications of that knowledge, form the young science of immunogenetics. In particular, producers must control diseases in their livestock if they are going to be profitable. While vaccines, hygiene, and other therapeutic methods control most diseases, vaccines are expensive and none of these methods is completely effective. However, there is evidence from experiments and field data of some degree of genetic control over the immune system in humans and animals. For example, bovine leukocyte adhesion deficiency (BLAD) is a hereditary disease that was discovered in Holstein calves in the 1980s. The presence of the BLAD gene leads to high rates of bacterial infections, pneumonia, diarrhea, and typically death by age four months in cattle, and those that survive their youth have stunted growth and continued susceptibility to infections. It was soon found that these calves carried two copies of a recessive gene that was present in nearly 25 percent of Holstein bulls. Cattle with only one copy of the gene, or carriers, had normal growth patterns and immune systems. Holstein bulls are now routinely tested for the BLAD gene before being used for artificial insemination. With a high percentage of Holsteins being bred artificially, a potentially major problem has been avoided.

Genetic control of the immune system is based on the DNA of the individuals. Histocompatibility genes that serve several functions are on one area of a chromosome, called the major histocompatibility complex (MHC), which exists in all higher vertebrates.

There are large numbers of genes involved in the MHCs of different species. There are more than 60 different alleles at one locus and other loci are multi-allelic. There are also differences among species in the number of genes known. In addition, selection experiments have demonstrated genetic variation between lines selected for high and low response to different antigens. Some vaccinations are more efficacious when the animals have been selected for resistance to the antigen for which they are vaccinated.

Substantial progress has been made in the field of immunogenetics, but limited use has been made of this knowledge. One reason for this is that immune systems have evolved to be generally robust. Changing the frequency of some genes that control immune function may inadvertently change the function of other genes and result in adverse effects. Experiments are now under way to determine whether sires' immune responses can be used to predict the health of their daughters under field conditions. The results indicate that there are differences among sires' daughter groups, but the differences are not large enough to control a high proportion of the variability. The tests used were based primarily on leukocytes, which are the first line of defense when an antigen invades an animal. Application of knowledge in the area of immunogenetics must be used with caution.

It might seem that integrating molecular markers and quantitative methods would be a trivial task. However, the effect of some genes depends on the presence of others, and these interactions need to be considered along with the particular breeding scheme. Furthermore, there are nongenetic influences that may turn genes on and off. Thus, some genes act individually, some genes interact, and the environment has a further impact. Finding how these all affect the phenotypic expression of an organism is complicated. However, this challenge presents an opportunity for future research and for producers.

Many advances in reproductive technologies have been made, though many are too expensive for everyday use. Most of the advanced techniques use artificial insemination, which was developed decades ago, though refinements continue.

GENETICALLY ENGINEERED (GE) ANIMALS

Because of the lengthy process of selective breeding which can require several generations to develop a desired trait, scientists began to use genetics to manipulate the characteristics of animals in the lab by doing gene transfers from other species that would produce desired traits in test subjects. The first gene transfers were done into mice in 1980. The resulting transgenic mice were carefully observed for issues with their development, with the appearance of disease, or motor function problems. The first transgenic sheep were reported just five years later by American scientist Robert E. Hammer and colleagues. The scientists' aim was to eventually create transgenic livestock with specific traits that benefited both farmers and consumers. However, more than thirty years after the first transgenic animals were created in the lab, there is still no approval from governing bodies like the FDA for the use of transgenic animals for human consumption. The results of this lack of approval, in some cases years after the approval was sought, have been tragic for some.

ENVIROPIGS

Researchers at the University of Guelph in Ontario genetically engineered a pig in the mid-1990s that could digest phosphorous compounds in its feed. As a result, the animal made manure with reduced phosphorus content, potentially leading to less pollution of groundwater beneath pig farms. The benefit to the environment seemed clear, as less groundwater pollution would also mean less pollution of groundwater-fed streams and lakes near pig. In 2007, the Enviropig, as the GM animal was called, was submitted for regulatory review by the U.S. government, and for review to the Canadian government in 2009. However, the approval process was halted. There had been an outcry against the Enviropig, based on concerns that the pigs might be enclosed in smaller facilities because there was

These Enviropigs are members of a trademarked genetically modified line of Yorkshire pigs. Developed at the University of Guelph, they can digest plant phosphorus more efficiently than conventional unmodified pigs.

less phosphorous in their manure. In 2010, the Department of the Environment of the Canadian Government determined that the Enviropig was in compliance with the Canadian Environmental Protection Act. However, several other applications concerning whether the animals were fit for human consumption had been submitted to other governing agencies, and none of those agencies had given approval. In April 2012, the program lost funding from its prime sponsor, Ontario Pork. Unable to get another financial backer, the researchers decided to euthanize the pigs that May, just days ahead of a planned effort to save the pigs' lives by a farm animal protection group. This was not the only animal rights group to attempt to help the pigs. Farm Sanctuary, a farm animal advocacy organization, offered to try to find homes for the pigs so that they could "live out their unnatural lives as naturally as possible." However, the university was unable to give the pigs away as doing so would breach Canadian regulations for the containment and use of transgenic animals. The main concern was that releasing the pigs could potentially put consumers at risk or harm the farming market. Though the project was officially over, genetic material from the Enviropig was stored at the Canadian Agricultural Genetics Repository Program.

GM SALMON

Another genetically modified animal that seemed to be on the fast-track to FDA approval was AquaBounty's AquAdvantage salmon. This salmon, an Atlantic salmon with one gene added from a Chinook salmon and one gene from an ocean pout, would grow in half the time it took wild salmon to grow and would consume a quarter less food. The fish, like other farm-raised fish, are all female and triploid, which meant that they were all sterile and unable to affect a natural or wild population

Genetically modified salmon in tanks at an AquaBounty GM salmon farm in Massachusetts.

of fish. Additionally, the fish were kept in indoor enclosures, so unless there was a catastrophic breach, there would be no way that the fish could intermingle with a wild population. The findings from the FDA were that there were no direct food consumption hazards. They also found there was no danger to wild salmon because of the protocols and precautions taken to keep the AquAdvantage salmon from wild fish.

However, an expert panel from the Royal Society of Canada which was set up in 2001, found that the introduction of growth hormone to transgenic salmon, notably Pacific and Atlantic salmon, created significant health and welfare problems for the fish. Whether those health and wellness concerns would transfer to humans who consume the fish remained unknown.

Despite the FDA's findings that the salmon was safe, it had not yet been approved for production or consumption.

ENRICHED MILK AND HORN-FREE COWS

Like the researchers at the University of Guelph, scientists who are pursuing the development of GM animals are facing an uphill battle to find funding. Some believe that an easier road to approval would be in milk from cows, goats, and sheep that is enriched through genetic engineering. In fact, some expect that milk will be the first food produced from GM animals to become available on the market. Because milk is external to the animal, scientists say it is easier to study. Chinese scientists using cows, and scientists at the University of California using goats, have enriched cow and goat milk with lysozyme. Lysozyme is produced at very high levels in human breast milk. However, the milk of goats and cows contain very little lysozyme. Lysozyme limits the growth of bacteria that can cause intestinal infections and diarrhea and is a main contributor in the health of human infants. The enriched milk was tested on pigs, and researchers found that the pigs that consumed lysozome-rich milk recovered much more quickly from infection and diarrhea. Scientists hope that this milk could be instrumental in lowering diarrheal diseases that affect young children in less-developed countries.

Creating a more nutrient-rich milk is not the only way that milk is being enhanced. Some researchers aim to increase the supply of milk by adding hormones that would produce more milk in less time to satisfy the demand of a growing world population, as well as lower the cost of milk—which can be an added benefit for people in less-developed countries. However, opponents to biotechnology-produced milk are concerned about the presence of bovine growth hormone (BGH), also sometimes called bovine somatotropin (bST). Scientists have developed techniques whereby bacteria can produce BGH/bST. While this can raise milk yields in cows, there is concern about what the growth hormone can do to a cow's body and whether some of those effects can translate to human consumers. BGH/bST increases metabolism, and stimulates bone and muscle growth in young animals. Research on cows that were bred naturally to produce more milk showed that the animals were also more susceptible to disease. BGH/bST cows

Dehorning cows (pictured) means less destruction and injury, but it is painful for the animal. Horn-free GM cows are being looked at as a solution.

could have the same problems, necessitating treatment with antibiotics, which would pose hazards to human consumers both through consumption of milk or the animal's meat. Synthetic BGH/bST has been banned in three Scandinavian countries and Canada.

A less concerning genetic modification is the creation of dairy cows that don't have any horns. Dairy farmers routinely dehorn or disbud their animals in order to reduce the risk of injury to farm workers, property, and other animals. Dehorned animals are easier to handle and transport, have a better resale value, and take up less trough space, making it possible for more animals to eat at the same time. The American Veterinary Medical Association recognizes that dehorning an animal causes pain, and recommends a variety of precautions including local anesthesia, sedation, and the administration of anti-inflammatories. Some scientists are working on a genetically modified cow that would not have any horns, eliminating all of these problems for both the animals and the farmers, as well as the expense involved in both handling the animals or as a result of any damage caused by the animal's horns. In this case, however, scientists are not tampering with genes from other animals. They are making changes to the animal's own DNA by tweaking the gene to create the desired trait. In this case, the genes of dairy cattle are being changed to match the genes of the hornless beef cattle in the hope that they too will be born without horns.

ARE SOME GE ANIMALS DIFFERENT?

Transgenic animals are produced in a slightly different way than animals that have their genomes "edited" as is the case with the horn-free cows previously mentioned. While transgenic animals have genes from different animals recombined with their own to produce new traits, animals that have their genomes edited are produced by modifying their own genes (rather than introducing foreign ones) and are basically the same as naturally-occurring animals because scientists are replicating a natural phenotype. The mutation that scientists are able to design could happen naturally through selective breeding, but it would take a very long time to achieve. Scientists hope that this more natural form of genetic modification would be more comfortable for consumers who are opposed to other types of genetic manipulation.

Both gene editing and the creation of transgenic animals through recombining DNA are different from another type of genetic modification: cloning. The FDA considers GE animals and clones to be different, and regulates GE animals differently from animal clones. The FDA has released their findings stating that there are no food safety risks associated with cloned animal, or the progeny of a clone. They consider a cloned animal to be as safe as a conventionally-bred animal. There are opponents to this finding, but to understand where both sides stand on the issue of cloned animals, it is important to understand the process of cloning.

CLONING

Cloning, an asexual method of reproduction, produces an individual with the same genetic material (DNA) as another individual. Probably the best-known examples of clones are identical twins, which result when cells in the early development stage separate and develop into different individuals. Though the DNA in cloned individuals is the same, environmental influences may make them differ in phenotype. Thus far, the commercial use of clones has been limited. Cloning can be used to produce clones from a highly productive individual, but the cost would have to be low enough to recover the expense quickly. Animals have been cloned by three processes: embryo splitting, blastomere dispersal, and nuclear transfer. Nuclear transfer is most common and involves enucleating an ovum, or egg, with all the genetic material removed. This material is replaced with a full set of chromosomes from a suitable donor cell, which is microinjected into the enucleated cell. Then the enucleated cell, with the transplanted chromosome, is placed into a recipient female to be carried through gestation.

CLONED FOOD

In 2008, the FDA released a statement saying that meat and milk from clones of cattle, swine, and goats, and the offspring of clones from any species traditionally consumed as food, are as safe to eat as food from conventionally bred animals. This finding was echoed by the European Food Safety Authority (EFSA) and the New Zealand Food Safety

Authority (NZFSA). However, organizations such as the Center for Food Safety point to the relatively new technology as imprecise and their results inconclusive. They warn that defects in these animals are common, which could lead to treatment with hormones and antibiotics which would then transfer to human consumers. Another concern raised is that of patenting breeds of animals by large corporations, which could put financial strain on small to medium-sized farms. Currently, there are no cloned animals being sold as food, however, cloned animals can be used as breeding stock. Their progeny could be sold at market for consumption. As yet, there are also no designer herds because the technology and methods required to produce large numbers of cloned animals remain prohibitively expensive. Some food safety advocates believe that food that comes from a cloned animal should be labeled, even if it is from a naturally-born animal whose parent is from cloned stock. Groups have lobbied government agencies for labeling that distinguishes cloned from naturally-produced animal meat. However, the FDA, NZFSA, EFSA, and FSA (Food Standards Agency in the UK) all feel that labeling is unnecessary as the food is equal to that from animals that are bred through conventional methods.

CHAPTER 4

PEST AND DISEASE CONTROL IN CROPS

F armers have been battling pests since the first plants were used for food. Several past pest attacks and infestations have had dramatic effects on human history, such as the Irish Potato Famine of 1845-49 which drastically affected Ireland's population. Farmers must manage their pest and disease problems or suffer the consequences of lower yields or reduced crop quality. The earliest farmers used crude forms of pest control, including removing each pest by hand—a labour-intensive approach, so the invention of pesticides were a great advantage to farmers, who could now treat a greater number of plants with minimal effort. Pesticides were invented to help curb potential problems, but they soon became the sources of other problems as the chemicals began to harm the environment, including consumers. The problem of pests, it seems, is a tricky one of balancing greater yield with safer food.

BEGINNINGS OF PEST CONTROL

Wherever agriculture has been practiced, pests have attacked, destroying part of or even the entire crop. In modern usage, the term pest includes animals (mostly insects), fungi, plants, bacteria, and viruses.

A farm worker sprays pesticide in a strawberry field.

Human efforts to control pests have a long history. Even in Neolithic times (about 7000 BCE), farmers practiced a crude form of biological pest control involving the more or less unconscious selection of seed from resistant plants. Severe locust attacks in the Nile Valley during the 13th century BCE are dramatically described in the Bible, and, in his *Natural History*, the Roman author Pliny the Elder describes picking insects from plants by hand and spraying. The scientific study of pests was not undertaken until the 17th and 18th centuries. The first successful large-scale conquest of a pest by chemical means was the control of the vine powdery mildew (*Uncinula necator*) in Europe in the 1840s. The disease, brought from the Americas, was controlled first by spraying with lime sulfur and, subsequently, by sulfur dusting.

Another serious epidemic was the potato blight that caused famine in Ireland in 1845 and some subsequent years and severe losses in many other parts of Europe and the United States. Insects and fungi from Europe became serious pests in the United States, too. Among these were the European corn borer, the gypsy moth, and the chestnut blight, which practically annihilated that tree.

The first book to deal with pests in a scientific way was John Curtis's *Farm Insects*, published in 1860. Though farmers were well aware that

THE IRISH POTATO FAMINE

The Irish Potato Famine, also called the Great Potato Famine, Great Irish Famine, or Famine of 1845–49, occurred in Ireland in 1845–49 when the potato crop failed in successive years. The crop failures were caused by late blight, a disease that destroys both the leaves and the edible roots, or tubers, of the potato plant. The causative agent of late blight is the water mold *Phytophthora infestans*. The Irish Potato Famine was the worst famine to occur in Europe in the 19th century.

By the early 1840s, almost one-half of the Irish population—but primarily the rural poor—had come to depend almost exclusively on the potato for their diet, and the rest of the population also consumed it in large quantities. A heavy reliance on just one or two high-yielding varieties of potato greatly reduced the genetic variety that ordinarily prevents the decimation of an entire crop by disease, and thus the Irish became vulnerable to famine. In 1845 *Phytophthora* arrived accidentally from North America, and that same year Ireland had unusually cool, moist weather, in which the blight thrived. Much of that year's potato crop rotted in the fields. This partial crop failure was followed by more devastating failures in 1846–49, as each year's potato crop was almost completely ruined by the blight.

The British government's efforts to relieve the famine were inadequate. Prime Minister Sir Robert Peel did what he could to provide relief in 1845 and early 1846, but under the Liberal cabinet of Lord John Russell, which assumed power in June 1846, the emphasis shifted to reliance on Irish resources and the free market, which made disaster inevitable. Much of the financial burden of providing for the starving Irish peasantry was thrown upon the Irish landowners themselves (through local poor relief). But because the peasantry was unable to pay its rents, the landlords soon ran out of funds with which to support them. British assistance was limited to loans, helping to fund soup kitchens, and providing employment on road building and other public works. Cornmeal imported from the United States helped

(*continued on the next page*)

Kerrs Pink potatoes, East Cork, County Cork, Ireland.

(continued from the previous page)

avert some starvation, but it was disliked by the Irish, and reliance on it led to nutritional deficiencies. Despite these shortcomings, by August 1847 as many as three million people were receiving rations at soup kitchens. All in all, the British government spent about £8 million on relief, and some private relief funds were raised as well. Throughout the famine, many Irish farms continued to export grain, meat, and other high-quality foods to Britain because the Irish peasantry lacked the money to purchase them. The government's grudging and ineffective measures to relieve the famine's distress intensified the resentment of British rule among the Irish people.

The famine proved to be a watershed in the demographic history of Ireland. As a direct consequence of the famine, Ireland's population of almost 8.4 million in 1844 had fallen to 6.6 million by 1851. The number of agricultural laborers and smallholders in the western and southwestern counties underwent an especially drastic decline. About one million people died from starvation or from typhus and other famine-related diseases. The number of Irish who immigrated during the famine may have reached two million. Ireland's population continued to decline in the following decades because of overseas immigration and lower birth rates. By the time Ireland achieved independence in 1921, its population was barely half of what it had been in the early 1840s.

insects caused losses, Curtis was the first writer to call attention to their significant economic impact. The successful battle for control of the Colorado potato beetle (*Leptinotarsa decemlineata*) of the western United

States also occurred in the 19th century. When miners and pioneers brought the potato into the Colorado region, the beetle fell upon this crop and became a severe pest, spreading steadily eastward and devastating crops, until it reached the Atlantic. It crossed the ocean and eventually established itself in Europe. But an American entomologist in 1877 found a practical control method consisting of spraying with water-insoluble chemicals such as London Purple, Paris green, and calcium and lead arsenates.

Other pesticides that were developed soon there after included nicotine, pyrethrum, derris, quassia, and tar oils, first used, albeit unsuccessfully, in 1870 against the winter eggs of the phylloxera plant louse. The Bordeaux mixture fungicide (copper sulfate and lime), discovered accidentally in 1882, was used successfully against vine downy mildew; this compound is still employed to combat it and potato blight. Since many insecticides available in the 19th century were comparatively weak, other pest-control methods were used as well. A species of ladybird beetle, *Rodolia cardinalis*, was imported from Australia to California, where it controlled the cottony-cushion scale then threatening to destroy the citrus industry. A moth introduced into Australia destroyed the prickly pear, which had made millions of acres of pasture useless for grazing. In the 1880s the European grapevine was saved from destruction by grape phylloxera through the simple expedient of grafting it onto certain resistant American rootstocks.

This period of the late 19th and early 20th centuries was thus characterized by increasing awareness of the possibilities of avoiding losses from pests, by the rise of firms specializing in pesticide manufacture, and by development of better application machinery.

PESTICIDES AS A PANACEA: 1942–62

In 1942 the Swiss chemist Paul Hermann Müller discovered the insecticidal properties of a synthetic chlorinated organic chemical, dichlorodiphenyltrichloroethane, which was first synthesized in 1874 and subsequently became known as DDT. Müller received the Nobel Prize for Physiology or Medicine in 1948 for his discovery. DDT was far more persistent and effective than any previously known insecticide. Originally a mothproofing agent for clothes, it soon found use among the armies of World War II for killing body lice and fleas. It stopped a typhus epidemic threatening Naples. Müller's work led to the discovery of other chlorinated insecticides, including aldrin, introduced in 1948; chlordane (1945); dieldrin (1948); endrin (1951); heptachlor (1948); methoxychlor (1945); and Toxaphene (1948).

Research on poison gas in Germany during World War II led to the discovery of another group of yet more powerful insecticides and acaricides (killers of ticks and mites)—the organophosphorus compounds, some of which had systemic properties; that is, the plant absorbed them without harm and became itself toxic to insects. The first systemic was octamethylpyrophosphoramide, trade named Schradan. Other organophosphorus insecticides of enormous power were also made, the most common being diethyl-p-nitrophenyl monothiophosphate, named parathion. Though low in cost, these compounds were toxic to humans and other warm-blooded animals. The products could poison by absorption through the skin, as well as through the mouth or lungs, thus, spray operators must wear respirators and special clothing. Systemic insecticides need not be carefully sprayed, however; the compound may be absorbed by watering the plant.

Though the advances made in the fungicide field in the first half of the 20th century were not as spectacular as those made with insecticides and herbicides, certain dithiocarbamates, methylthiuram disulfides, and thaladimides were found to have special uses. It began to seem that almost any pest, disease, or weed problem could be mastered by suitable chemical treatment. Farmers foresaw a pest-free millennium. Crop losses were cut sharply; locust attack was reduced to a manageable problem; and the new chemicals, by killing carriers of human disease, saved the lives of millions of people.

Problems appeared in the early 1950s. In cotton crops standard doses of DDT, parathion, and similar pesticides were found ineffective and had to be doubled or trebled. Resistant races of insects had developed. In addition, the powerful insecticides often destroyed natural predators and helpful parasites along with harmful insects. Insects and mites can reproduce at such a rapid rate that often when natural predators were destroyed by a pesticide treatment, a few pest survivors from the treatment, unchecked in breeding, soon produced worse outbreaks of pests than there had been before the treatment; sometimes the result was a population explosion to pest status of previously harmless insects.

At about the same time, concern also began to be expressed about the presence of pesticide residues in food, humans, and wildlife. It was found that many birds and wild mammals retained considerable quantities of DDT in their bodies, accumulated along their natural food chains. The disquiet caused by this discovery was epitomized in 1962 by the publication in the United States of a book entitled *Silent Spring*, whose author, Rachel Carson, attacked the indiscriminate use of pesticides, drew attention to various abuses, and stimulated a reappraisal of pest control. Thus began a new "integrated" approach, which was in effect a return to the use of all methods of control in place of a reliance on chemicals alone.

INTEGRATED CONTROL

Some research into biological methods to control crop and herd pests was undertaken by governments, and in

RACHEL CARSON'S *SILENT SPRING*

Silent Spring is a nonfiction book written by Rachel Carson that became one of the most-influential books in the modern environmental movement. Published in 1962, *Silent Spring* was widely read by the general public and became a *New York Times* best seller. The book provided the impetus for tighter control of pesticides and has been honored on many lists of influential books, including *Discover* magazine's list of the 25 greatest science books of all time. The title *Silent Spring* was inspired by a line from the John Keats poem "La Belle Dame sans Merci" and evokes a ruined environment in which "the sedge is wither'd from the lake, / And no birds sing."

Carson was a biologist and science writer who earned a master's degree in zoology from Johns Hopkins University in Baltimore, Maryland, in 1932. Following the success of her second book, *The Sea Around Us* (1951), she quit her job with the Bureau of Fisheries in 1952 to concentrate on her writing career. Although she had been aware of the use of synthetic pesticides since World War II (when DDT was widely used to control malaria and typhus), she did not concentrate on the topic until 1957, when she was recruited by the National Audubon Society to investigate the dangers of the loosely regulated use of DDT and other pesticides. In addition to reading scientific literature and attending Food and Drug Administration hearings on the use of chemical pesticides on food crops, Carson conducted extensive interviews with scientists and physicians to learn about the effects of pesticides.

(continued on the next page)

Rachel Carson.

(*continued from the previous page*)

Silent Spring was first published as a serial in the *New Yorker* and then as a book by Houghton Mifflin. Documenting the many harmful effects pesticides have on the environment, Carson argued that pesticides should properly be called "biocides" because of their impact on organisms other than the target pests. Specifically, she noted the harm DDT inflicted on bird populations and warned of a future spring characterized by the lack of birdsong. She highlighted the fact that DDT was classified as a chemical carcinogen implicated in causing liver tumors in mice and accused representatives of the chemical industry of spreading disinformation contradicted by scientific research. She also accused government officials of uncritically accepting the chemical industry's claims of safety and, more radically, questioned the then-dominant paradigm of scientific progress and the philosophical belief that man was destined to exert control over nature. She argued that the success of pesticides is necessarily limited because the target pests tend to develop immunity, while risks to humans and the environment will increase as the pesticides accumulate in the environment. However, *Silent Spring* did not call for the cessation of all pesticide use; it called for greater moderation and care in their use.

Upon publication of *Silent Spring*, Carson was attacked as an alarmist and was accused of trying to reverse scientific progress. The chemical industry mounted a counterattack and presented the book as an example of how an overzealous reformer can stir up public opinion and militate for the passage of regulations that ultimately do more harm than good. However, Carson's claims were vindicated in an investigation ordered by U.S. President John F. Kennedy, which led to an immediate strengthening of regulations regarding the use of chemical pesticides.

Although Rachel Carson died in 1964, *Silent Spring* remained influential far beyond her lifetime. It was persuasive in campaigns against the use of DDT, which was banned in the United States in 1972 and internationally in 2004 except when used for the control of malaria-causing mosquitoes. The book also provided a model of radical environmental activism that questioned prevailing attitudes about the benefits of scientific progress and the attitude that humans should take toward nature.

many countries plant breeders began to develop and patent new pest-resistant plant varieties.

One method of biological control involved the breeding and release of males sterilized by means of gamma rays. Though sexually potent, such insects have inactive sperm. Released among the wild population, they mate with the females, who either lay sterile eggs or none at all. The method was used with considerable success against the screwworm, a pest of cattle, in Texas. A second method of biological control employed lethal genes. It is sometimes possible to introduce a lethal or weakening gene into a pest population, leading to the breeding of intersex (effectively neuter) moths or a predominance of males. Various studies have also been made on the chemical identification of substances attracting pests to the opposite sex or to food. With such substances traps can be devised that attract only a specific pest species. Finally, certain chemicals have been fed to insects to sterilize them. Used in connection with a food lure, these can lead to the elimination of a pest from an area. Chemicals tested so far, however, have been considered too dangerous to humans and other mammals for any general use.

Some countries (notably the United States, Sweden, and the United Kingdom) have partly or wholly banned the use of DDT because of its persistence and accumulation in human body fat and its effect on wildlife. New pesticides of lesser human toxicity

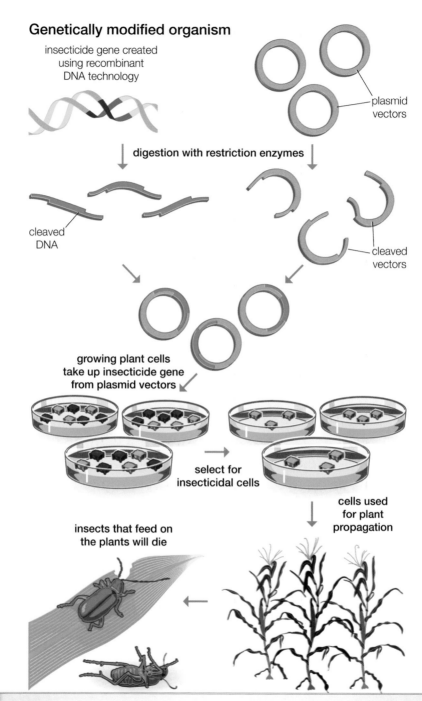

Genetically modified organism

insecticide gene created
using recombinant
DNA technology

plasmid
vectors

digestion with restriction enzymes

cleaved
DNA

cleaved
vectors

growing plant cells
take up insecticide gene
from plasmid vectors

select for
insecticidal cells

cells used
for plant
propagation

insects that feed on
the plants will die

Genetically modified organisms, such as plants engineered to be toxic to plant-feeding insects, are produced using scientific methods that include recombinant DNA technology.

have been found, one of the most used being mercap-tosuccinate, trade named Malathion. A more recent important discovery was the systemic fungicide, absorbed by the plant and transmitted throughout it, making it resistant to certain diseases.

The majority of pesticides are sprayed on crops as solutions or suspensions in water. Spraying machinery has developed from the small hand syringes and "garden engines" of the 18th century to the very powerful "autoblast machines" of the 1950s that were capable of applying up to some 400 gallons per acre (4,000 liters per hectare). Though spraying suspended or dissolved pesticide was effective, it involved moving a great quantity of inert material for only a relatively small amount of active ingredient. Low-volume spraying was invented about 1950, particularly for the application of herbicides, in which 10 or 20 gallons of water, transformed into fine drops, would carry the pesticide. Ultralow-volume spraying has also been introduced; 4 ounces (about 110 grams) of the active ingredient itself (usually Malathion) are applied to an acre from aircraft. The spray as applied is invisible to the naked eye.

THE ORGANIC FOOD MOVEMENT

Backlash from consumers about the use of pesticides and the effect of these chemicals on the environment as well as concern regarding the safety of GM animals has encouraged an organic food movement. Some farmers today feel strongly about an alternative to chemical fertilizers and pesticides, preferring organic farming which uses techniques that had been implemented by farmers centuries ago. Organic farming as a conscious rejection of modern agri-chemical techniques had its origin in the 1930s, when Sir Albert Howard, a British agricultural scientist, introduced a system of holistic and natural animal and plant husbandry in which town wastes were returned to the soil for utilization as nutrient material.

This system's end product is organic food. Its popularity has risen and fallen over the years with its most recent incarnation in the United States as what the *New York Times* dubbed a "food revolution" in a 2009 article. Advocates of organic and locally grown food were enjoying sympathetic ears in politics for the first time in years. First Lady Michelle Obama made a point to highlight the importance of fresh, unprocessed food, and created a White House vegetable garden. But by 2011, only 0.6 percent of total cropland and pasture in the United States was certified organic. Organic food and beverages made up over 4 percent of the national market and were sold in nearly 20,000 markets as well as three out of four national groceries as of 2014.

ORGANIC FARMING

Common reasons for undertaking organic farming are concerns for the environment, the amount of

Different varieties of organic lettuce.

chemicals used in nonorganic farming, and the amount of energy required in agriculture. Many chemicals used on farms are manufactured using large amounts of fossil fuels. Finally, farmers may find organic agriculture to be both personally satisfying and profitable.

Central ideas of organic farming include crop rotations, growing crops called cover crops that enrich the soil, and balanced host and predator rela-

tionships. Any grains, forages, and protein supplements fed to livestock must be organically grown. Farms produce organic residues and nutrients that are then recycled back into the soil. In addition to cover crops, composted manure is used to maintain soil fertility.

Where chemical fertilizers feed plants directly, the organic farming system employs organic materials such as animal manure, compost, grass turf, straw, and other similar materials to improve soil structure and health.

Pests are controlled through prevention methods such as diversified farming, crop rotation, and growing crop varieties with natural resistance to pests and disease. Sterile male insects and predators of pests are introduced into the environment as well. Pest management includes using products that are part of the Allowed Substances List for organic farming as listed in the Code of Federal Regulations. The products meet organic standards and are considered "natural" methods of pest control.

Organic farming provides an alternative production method for farmers, but it also introduces its own set of challenges. Generally, organic farms are small-scale and labor intensive. While nearly every crop can be grown organically, not all commodities are equally easy or challenging. Transitioning from traditional to organic farming is difficult, costly, and takes time. There are a number of demanding requirements that organic farmers must meet for 36 months before harvesting the first crop. During these months, products do not qualify as "certified organic" and cannot be sold at more profitable prices. New organic farmers have developed methods such as growing crops with lost cost production while transitioning. Lost cost production involves growing low-cost crops that can't be sold at premium prices, but allow farmers to more cheaply make the transition to certified organic crops. But rules such as those prohibiting parallel production—growing organic and conventional products simultaneously—adds constraints.

STANDARDS

Organic farmers must meet certain criteria to be officially considered organic. With the growth of the organic market, the government stepped in to help verify that products advertised as organic meet a certain standard. More than 40 private organizations and state agencies have the power to certify what food is organic and what is not. However, their standards are not all the same. A pesticide or fertilizer prohibited by one organization may be permissible by another. In the late 1980s, the organic industry petitioned Congress to define what organic meant as part of the Organic Foods Production Act. The act requires the secretary of Agriculture to create a list of allowed and prohibited substances that can and cannot be used in organic food production and handling operations.

While also setting a set of national standards organic foods must meet, the act also requires the USDA to establish an organic certification program. The program follows recommendations by the National Organic Standards Board as well as certification programs in place at the state, private, and foreign levels.

The National Standards on Organic Agricultural Production and Handling (National Organic Program or NOP rule) was issued in December of 2000, and set more standards organic food producers must meet. Requirements address organic crop production, wild crop harvesting, organic livestock management, and organic food processing. Various accreditation requirements must be met and compliance and testing fees paid. The NOP rule specifically addresses and prohibits ionizing radiation, sewage sludge, and genetic engineering or modification.

Other methods or techniques organic standards generally prohibit include animal cloning, synthetic pesticides, synthetic fertilizers, and synthetic food processing aids and ingredients. Additionally, no prohibited products or practices can be used on an organic farm for at least three years prior to harvest. Livestock must be raised organically and fed 100 percent organic food.

FARM-TO-TABLE

Today consumers are able to purchase a variety of fruits, vegetables, and other agricultural products regardless of whether the foods are able to be grown domestically or not. Different products, like bananas, coffee, chocolate, nuts, spices, and fish, are imported into the United States. This is because of globalization, which is an integration among people of different countries around the world. Many look at the food production system or supply chain as part of a continuum with food globalization on one end, and what is known as farm-to-table on the other end of the continuum. The modern farm-to-table movement, sometimes referred to as farm-to-fork, or the locavore movement, promotes locally grown crops and agriculture. Farmers sell directly to the consumer, either through sales at farmers' markets for small farms, or by allowing consumers to come to the farm for medium-sized farms.

Proponents of farm-to-table claim that selling directly to consumers can help address issues such as obesity, which can be partially blamed on the amount of sugar in processed foods available at most supermarkets. It can also increase the availability of healthy food options in poor, urban neighbourhoods. Because farm-to-table foods are locally sourced, the costs of packaging, shipping, and refrigeration are very low. The farm-to-table movement would create demand for local products which benefits both the farmers and their communities, and would increase sustainability, a method of farming that does not completely use up or destroy natural resources. Farm-to-table advocate organizations help local farmers become educated about advances in agricultural techniques while also providing them with technologies to become more sustainable and profitable. Finally, it has been claimed that the farm-to-table movement can help raise public awareness of environmental, social, and health issues.

Some farms have taken to inviting customers to dinner where they are served meals created by local chefs and grown by their local farmer, who sits with guests at the dinner table. A farm in New Hampshire serves meat from pasture-fed pigs for dinner. Another farm in Minnesota includes bluegrass music while diners use compostable tableware. Some give tours of the farm, and farmers give an explanation of the ingredients being served with each course.

The benefit of this approach is that it makes local chefs important members of their community, while the local food producers become more involved with providing meals to residents at festivals and children at school (farm-to-school). The food, delivery, and minimal processing are all sustainable, and the food supply is reliable.

While many feel more comfortable with the farm-to-table movement as they look for more sustainable sources of food that do not include those that come from large industrial farms, some feel that this organic movement misses the mark. Chef Dan Barber argues that chefs treat local farmers like grocery stores, only choosing what they most want to use. However, he feels that to really support these farmers and this particular type of farming, it is incumbent on the chef to use what the farmer grows when it is grown, rather than waiting for the one crop that they really want. Some farmers recognize that they may have only a limited number of cash crops, but in order to prepare the soil for that crop, they have to grow other things throughout the year. Some of the crops grown are used as animal feed, rather than being eaten by people. Barber thinks that chefs should do more work to ensure that people are eating everything the farmer produces.

Other chefs feel that the farm-to-table movement has gone too far. These food professionals say that the "save the world" mentality is not for chefs and that the term farm-to-table has become overused and abused, and may have lost its original meaning. Ultimately, their belief is that chefs are supposed to make delicious food, and anything else beyond that distracts from the final goal. One of their concerns is that following the farm-to-table method requires too much effort from the chef. It takes a lot of time and effort to find quality food producers within a certain budget. Chefs have to make it their mission to find the best farmer, forager, fisherman, pig man, egg farmer, or any other food producer in a local network. It also takes time to build relationships with farmers, producers, and purveyors. This, they believe, takes away from time best used for actual cooking.

URBAN AND LOCAL GARDENS

While farm-to-table is supposed to provide better and more nutritious food to urban locations, produce from small to medium-sized farms can be considerably more expensive than those from industrial farms that use the methods and techniques that proponents of organic food are against. The question of cost, nutrition, sustainability, and availability is one that is being addressed in new and creative ways.

In Sacramento, California, residents are turning empty lots into small farms. As an extension of the farm-to-fork movement, farms are being established inside city limits as opposed to a remote location away from the majority of the population. The plan, in addition to making fresh crops available to urban areas, helps clean up the city. Local Sacramento gardener Paul Trudeau transformed an empty lot into one that produces food.

He commented on the condition of the lot, "This was a mess back here; it had an old dryer, had an old bed."

Currently, unless the land is legally designated as agricultural, small urban farms located in residential, commercial, or industrial zones are prohibited from selling locally grown crops. Trudeau is one of many hoping to change the laws to allow urban farms to sell their products. This is just one of the myriad roadblocks facing urban and local gardens today.

Large-scale farms qualify for agricultural tax relief, a benefit that urban and small-scale farms do not enjoy. In many counties, definitions of agricultural land use exclude these small farms and gardens. One small-scale farmer who did not qualify for agricultural exemptions saw his property tax rate rise 800 percent in one year.

In Texas, inconsistent local health regulations are confusing. It is difficult for farmers and chefs to know which foods are permitted, which require a permit, and which they can sell and distribute. Locally produced foods may also be restricted from sale. One home-based bakery owner noted that five minutes after she opened her doors to sell homemade pies, a city employee shut the operation down. In Texas, one law on local products allows farmers to sell unpasteurized milk at the location where it is produced, but nowhere else. Lawmakers cite health safety and concerns as reasons to have such regulations. It is the same concerns over health and safety that drive consumers away from GM crops and food. Farmers argue that these restrictions make it

Urban gardens are one type of small-scale farming that brings fresh produce to urban markets. However, they have been legally challenged.

difficult for potential customers to access their product. There are efforts to widen the scope of local and urban farms, but the public health debate is far from over.

A WORLDWIDE SOLUTION?

High expectations and hopes have been pinned to organic farming and foods. A UN report in 2013 titled "Trade and Environment Review 2013: Wake Up

Before It's Too Late" compiled the opinions of more than 60 experts around the world to support a change in conventional food, agriculture, and trade systems. The report recommended a shift toward local small-scale farmers and food systems, diversifying farms, and reducing the use of fertilizer.

The report also supported reforming global trade rules to accomplish these goals. Counter to their recommendations, there are laws in place that strengthen multinational corporate and financial firms over the local farmer.

However, just one year prior, there were already questions about the viability of the organic farm movement. Producers have supplemented their produce with processed options such as jams and juice, but these do not always meet fresh market standards. Fruit and vegetable crops are challenging to grow for organic farmers. Certain pests are very difficult to address only through organic methods. Yields of organic horticultural crops are generally less than non-organic crops yields. Organic agriculture produces decent yields for crops like beans or fruit trees, but organic farming delivers up to 25 percent less yield for crops like corn, wheat, and broccoli.

As the world population rapidly increases, there is a demand for more food and methods of farming that can accommodate a greater number of people. Critics of organic farming see conventional farming methods and use of GMOs as the only reasonable option. Genetically altering plants to grow year-round can address the need for more crops.

Like most complex problems, experts believe that the solution will not be simple. The ideal farming method may vary from location to location and even from crop to crop. Organic farming does increase soil health, and this is key to better agriculture regardless of overall method. Experts note that current conventional agriculture degrades natural resources and harms the land in the long term. Their recommendations include considering hybrid forms of agriculture that combines conventional with organic systems.

CHAPTER 5

ECONOMICS, POLITICS, AND GMOs

A griculture has always been influenced by the actions of governments around the world. Never was this more evident than during the first half of the 20th century, when two major wars profoundly disrupted food production. In response to the tumultuous economic climate, European countries implemented tariffs and other measures to protect local agriculture. Such initiatives had global ramifications, and by the mid-20th century various international organizations had been established to monitor and promote agricultural development and the well-being of rural societies.

PRODUCTION: TOO MUCH, TOO LITTLE

There is a great range in agricultural production around the world. Some countries, using high technology and advanced methods, produce more through agriculture than they need or can use, while others—underdeveloped and poorer—never produce enough to sustain their populations.

Big farms use heavy machinery like these combine harvesters to meet large-scale demands for a growing world population.

Countries with more advanced agriculture often attempt to help underdeveloped areas improve farm productivity. This aid is often invaluable, but sometimes questionable for the long term. Agricultural systems are intimately connected to places and peoples. Propelling such areas into modern agricultural cropping techniques may be a shock to the local culture. In some cases, advanced technologies may not be advisable under the climatic and soil conditions of the area. The native method is often a marvel of ingenuity developed over many generations through intimate contact with a unique situation. There may be no bumper crops, but the wonder is that there is any crop at all.

Many countries in the Western Hemisphere consistently produce more food than they use. The surpluses are stored in granaries and warehouses for later use or sale to other countries. Storing the surpluses costs money because giant bins and huge buildings must be built and maintained. Techniques for reducing spoilage and loss to pests add to the cost.

As farmers continue to seek the greatest possible yield for the most reasonable cost, advanced agriculture is becoming as elaborate and as complicated as other modern industries. In the United States and in other wealthy countries where population is not yet a burden, the cost of labour is relatively high and is the limiting factor in production. Thus there has been more and more mechanization and automation.

FEEDING THE WORLD

There are more than 820 million people in the world who are chronically hungry. Most live in sub-Saharan Africa, Southern Asia, and Latin America.

Trying to produce enough food to keep up with the ever-increasing global population is probably agriculture's biggest challenge. By 2030 an additional two billion people will need to be fed, using the same fragile land and water resources that are available now.

A woman in Melmoth, KwaZulu-Natal, South Africa, hoeing a corn field. This type of small-scale farming, called agroecology, could help to stave off hunger in developing countries.

Even in developed countries, many people do not have reliable access to food. In 2012, 17.6 million American households (roughly one in seven) were food insecure at some time during the year. In 2005, that number was about 12.6 million.

Distributing agricultural surpluses from regions of bountiful production to areas suffering from food shortages seems an ideal solution. But it is far more difficult than it seems. The surpluses currently produced by agriculturally advanced countries are often given to school lunch programs, to families on public assistance, and to welfare institutions within the countries themselves. Food and fibre crops are sold abroad for foreign currencies to improve the producing country's balance of trade.

Even if the food could be easily distributed to other countries, the costs for transporting it run high. Some countries may complain that others ruin their markets by giving a commodity away or selling it at cut-rate prices. These problems, too, must be carefully weighed against the benefits to poorer countries.

GOVERNMENT'S ROLE

Because agriculture has been considered important to a country's well-being, governments have often been concerned with supporting it. Farmers face many risks that can dramatically change their incomes from year to year, and governments have often stepped in with programs to help stabilize farm incomes. The United States and Canada have a long history of such programs for agriculture. Currently, the United States provides price and income support programs for grains, oilseeds, fibres, dairy products, sugar, and a few other crops. Over the last two decades, the traditional reliance on keeping prices high through government purchases of commodities and restrictions on production or imports has given way to a greater reliance on providing support payments directly to farmers. This change allows farm products to sell at world prices, helping U.S. farmers participate in expanding global markets. It also allows them to produce what they think will bring them the highest returns, instead of what government programs require.

U.S. agricultural policy also includes programs to help producers recover from disasters, market products more effectively, and farm in ways that preserve or enhance the environment. Over the years programs have also been added to help rural communities promote economic development and to make food more available to low-income Americans, children, and the elderly.

An example of the government's lending a helping hand to both farmers and the environment is the U.S. Department of Agriculture's (USDA's) Conservation Reserve Program (CRP). The CRP offers technical and financial assistance to farmers trying to address soil, water, and other natural-resource-related issues on their lands. The program encourages farmers to convert environmentally sensitive acreage to healthy vegetative cover, such as native grasses, wildlife plantings, trees, or riparian buffers. Farmers receive an annual rental payment for committing their lands in this way.

The European Economic Community (EEC) established a Common Agricultural Policy (CAP) for its member countries, called the Common Market countries. The aim is to create free trade for individual commodities within the community. When production of a commodity exceeds EEC consumption, the EEC may buy the excess for storage, pay to have it reprocessed, or export it to countries outside the Common Market. In this way the EEC can maintain its members' farm prices at levels equal to or even higher than those in such market-competitive countries as the United States and Canada.

FROM "GREEN REVOLUTION" TO "GENE REVOLUTION"

Starting in the late 1960s, two forces merged that had a tremendous effect on the productivity of global agriculture. First, scientists found ways to grow more-vigorous, high-yielding crops. Better and more fertilizer helped increase the amount of crops harvested from the same plot of land. Plant breeding became a major method for increasing crop yields. Wheat farmers, for example, knew that key ingredients to better harvests were water availability and responsiveness to soil fertility. To a lesser extent but still integral to the final result was plant resistance to disease from fungal pathogens and other factors. Knowing this, research programs focused on control of water, soil fertility, and plant disease for wheat breeding. Other traits breeders looked for included weed competition resistance, ability to withstand insects, and overall appearance. Agriculture was irreversibly affected by the introduction of cheap nitrogen in the form of synthetic manures used for fertilization. Fixed nitrogen was found to be so effective yet available at such low costs that agricultural producers became completely dependent on it. The new invention affected plant breeders as well, since they had to now assume heavy nitrogen fertilization would be part of the plant's environment.

The second force that had a major effect on global agriculture was when international programs and foundations stepped forward to bring these improved crop varieties and technologies (such as proper fertilizer usage) to farmers in less-developed countries. The aim was to make the knowledge available to every crop producer around the world by 1980. The changes in less-developed countries were astonishing.

As a result of the intervention of these programs,

cDNA library

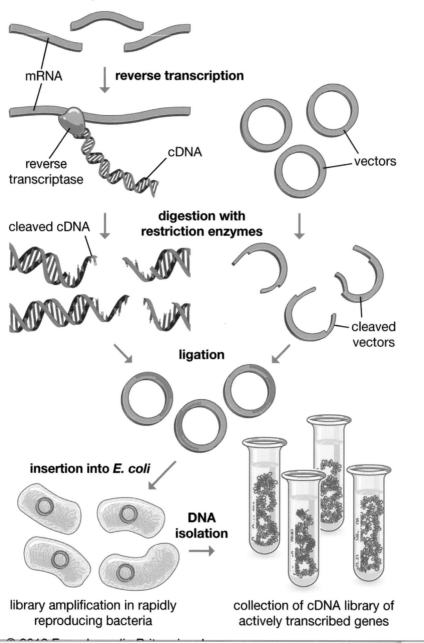

mRNA

reverse transcription

reverse transcriptase

cDNA

vectors

cleaved cDNA

digestion with restriction enzymes

cleaved vectors

ligation

insertion into E. coli

DNA isolation

library amplification in rapidly reproducing bacteria

collection of cDNA library of actively transcribed genes

A cDNA library represents a collection of only the genes that are encoded into proteins by an organism. This makes it easier to make proteins for cellular analysis, and more precision in the creation of GMOs staple grains were feeding more people than they ever had. In less-developed countries, wheat yields rose by 200 percent, corn by 150 percent, and rice by over 100 percent. This introduction into less-developed countries of new strains of wheat and rice was a major aspect of what became known as the Green Revolution. Given adequate water and ample amounts of the required chemical fertilizers and pesticides, these varieties have resulted in significantly higher yields.

Improvements brought about by traditional breeding techniques were largely responsible for spurring the Green Revolution. But today, in light of increasing global population growth, many researchers point to biotechnology as a source of great promise for feeding the world. Poorer farmers, however, often have not been able to provide the required growing conditions and therefore have obtained even lower yields with "improved" grains than they had gotten with the older strains that were better adapted to local conditions and that had some resistance to pests and diseases.

In 1972, Herbert W. Boyer, PhD, a faculty member at the University of California San Diego, met with Stanley N. Cohen, MD, a faculty member at Stanford, to discuss DNA found in *E. coli* bacteria. They were interested in how extrachromosomal DNA called plasmils could confer resistance to different antibiotics. They isolated pieces of DNA from animals, bacteria, and viruses, then tied these pieces together in a small plasmid from *E. coli*. What happened next sparked the genetic revolution.

The world's first recombinant DNA was introduced back into *E. coli* bacteria. The cells expressed not only the normal plasmid genes, but also those from the animals, other bacteria, and viruses that were artificially inserted. For their work with recombinant DNA, Cohen and Boyer were awarded the Nobel Prize.

Advances in human understanding of microorganisms, plants, livestock, and the environment have caused an increase in the number of biotechnology products. Using the tools of biotechnology, scientists have been able to introduce specific, desirable genes into plants and animals, thereby endowing crops with built-in insect resistance and herbicide tolerance. As previously discussed, this science is also being used to make important global foods, including rice (such as "golden rice") and cassava, more nutritious. This is critical, as vitamin deficiencies, particularly vitamin A and iron deficiencies, are prevalent across the less-developed regions of the world. The new proteins and biochemical pathways being discovered in research labs can be incorporated into crops and animals, allowing those species to perform new functions. Through biotechnology, people are able to produce more food per acre. In South Africa, small-scale farmers who incorporated novel biotechnologies saw larger financial benefits despite paying lower technology fees (the price for access to genetically modified seeds). They were even enjoying more benefits than their large-scale counterparts. Large dryland farmers saw a 14 percent yield increase while small-scale dryland farmers enjoyed increases between 16 and 40 percent from 1998 to 2000.

The first commercially grown genetically modified crop, a type of transgenic tobacco developed for seed multiplication, was made available in China in 1992. The Flavr Savr tomato was grown commercially for food in the United States beginning in 1994. By 1996, 1.45 million hectares (3.58 million acres) worldwide were growing genetically modified soy, corn, and cotton. By 2007 about half of the total global area dedicated to genetically modified crops was in the United States. Many other countries, such as Argentina, Canada, China, India, Mexico, and the Philippines, would adopt the new agricultural method. Each country's government has its own set of priorities regarding crops. China has focused on crops with the highest potential gains. Cotton, in particular, accounts for 5 million to 6 million hectares (1.23 million to 1.48 million acres) and 4 percent of total crop area. Priority in China is also given to rice, wheat, corn, soybean, potato, and rapeseed.

Many people are involved in creating newer versions of crops. Soil scientists, fertilizer chemists, hydrologists, irrigation specialists, entomologists, and plant pathologists all played a role in ushering in a new era of agriculture. But key to genetic modification were the plant breeders who could select the precise plant varieties that would produce the highest yields.

Beyond food production, biotechnology has introduced antioxidants into beauty products, and made more human physiology-compatible medicines, among other things. But where chemicals are used, concern has been voiced about their cost—since they generally must be imported—and about their potentially harmful effects on the environment. Efforts have been made to address these concerns. As previously discussed, farms that wish to be certified organic, must meet strict regulations to avoid contaminating their organic products with genetically modified foods. However, questions still remain regarding the long-term effects on people and the environment from the use of biotech products.

GENETICALLY MODIFIED FOODS IN THE FIGHT AGAINST HUNGER

In order to provide more food to the places that need it most, and a maximum of nutrition to nutrition-deficient populations, GMOs were introduced to traditional agriculture.

GM foods were first approved for human consumption in the United States in 1994, and by 1999 almost 50 percent of the corn, cotton, and

A corn earworm eating corn. Limiting damage from pests is a compelling reason behind the development of GM crops.

soybeans planted in the United States were GM. By the end of 2010, GM crops covered more than 9.8 million square kilometers (3.8 million square miles) of land in 29 countries worldwide—one-tenth of the world's farmland.

The use of engineered crops has reduced the need for application of wide-spectrum insecticides in many areas growing plants, such as potatoes, cotton, and corn, that were endowed with a gene from the

MONSANTO COMPANY

Monsanto Company has been at the forefront of the current pushback against GM foods: Most notably, they have been against the movement to label foods that are genetically modified, owing to the fact that their primary focus is in developing GM seeds. However, the company did not get its start in biotechnology. The Monsanto Chemical Works was founded in 1901 by John F. Queeny (1859–1933), a purchasing agent for a wholesale drug company, to manufacture the synthetic sweetener saccharin, then produced only in Germany. Queeny invested $1,500 of his own money and borrowed another $3,500 from a local Epsom salts manufacturer to launch his new company, which he named Monsanto, after his wife's maiden name. The firm was up to full-scale saccharin production in 1902, added caffeine and vanillin to its product line over the next few years, and in 1905 began turning a profit. With the Coca-Cola Company as one of Monsanto's chief customers, sales reached $1 million in 1915. Monsanto began producing aspirin in 1917.

Like many other American chemical companies, Monsanto expanded during World War I and flourished under the protection of the high U.S. tariffs of the 1920s. Queeny passed control of the company to his son, Edgar M. Queeny (1897–1968), in 1928. Edgar Queeny transformed Monsanto into an industrial giant before he retired in 1960. The company was incorporated as the Monsanto Chemical Company in 1933. Its production of styrene, a component of synthetic rubber, was vital to the U.S. war effort during World War II. Reflecting its diverse product offerings, the company changed its name to Monsanto Company in 1964. In 1985 Monsanto purchased pharmaceutical firm G.D. Searle & Co., maker of the NutraSweet artificial sweetener. Monsanto sold its sweeteners businesses, including NutraSweet, in 2000.

In the 1990s Monsanto's acquisition of Calgene Inc., DEKALB Genetics, and other biotechnology firms made it a leader in the development and production of genetically modified crop seeds. It began commercial production of BST (bovine somatotropin), a synthetic supplement for dairy cows, in 1994. Monsanto merged with global pharmaceutical company Pharmacia & Upjohn in March 2000, but in August 2002 Monsanto's nonpharmaceutical segments were spun off by Pharmacia Corporation, and Monsanto became a publicly traded company. Its primary businesses are in agriculture and biotechnology.

bacterium *Bacillus thuringiensis*, which produces a natural insecticide called Bt toxin. Field studies conducted in India in which Bt cotton was compared with non-Bt cotton demonstrated a 30–80 percent increase in yield from the GM crop. This increase was attributed to marked improvement in the GM plants' ability to overcome bollworm infestation, which was otherwise common. Studies of Bt cotton production in Arizona, demonstrated only small gains in yield—about 5 percent—with an estimated cost reduction of $25–65 (USD) per acre due to decreased pesticide applications. In China, a seven-year study of farms planting Bt cotton demonstrated initial success of the GM crop, with farmers who had planted Bt cotton reducing their pesticide use by 70 percent and increasing their earnings by 36 percent. However, after four years, the benefits of Bt cotton eroded as populations of insect pests other than bollworm increased, and farmers once again were forced to spray broad-spectrum pesticides. While the problem was not Bt-resistant bollworms, as had been feared initially, it nonetheless became clear that much more research was needed for communities to realize sustainable and environmentally responsible benefits from planting GM crops.

Other GM plants were engineered for resistance to a specific chemical herbicide, rather than resistance to a natural predator or pest. Herbicide-resistant crops (HRC) have been available since the mid-1980s; these crops enable effective chemical control of weeds, since only the HRC plants can survive in fields treated with the corresponding herbicide. However, the crops had an undesired side-effect when weeds became resistant to the herbicide. Farmers then returned to glyphosphate-based herbicides, which were the norm before GM plants, but certain weeds developed resistance to those as well. One weed in particular—pigweed—became resistant in about four years, and because the weed can grow more than 2.5 inches (6.3 centimeters) a day and produce 600,000 seeds, it became a nearly unstoppable infestation. Farmers increased application of chemicals to the soil, rather than decreased application in order to control the "superweed." The solution from scientists and corporations is to develop other types of HRCs that are resistant to more than one herbicide, but opponents argue that this will likely only create more superweeds. In an editorial piece published in the scientific journal *Nature* in 2014, the writer made the following argument:

> Stacking up tolerance traits may delay the appearance of resistant weeds, but probably not for long. Weeds are wily: farmers have already reported some plants that are resistant to more than five herbicides. And with glyphosate-resistant weeds already in many fields, the chances of preventing resistance to another are dropping.

By 2002 more than 60 percent of processed foods consumed in the United States contained at least some GM ingredients. Despite the concerns of some consumer groups, especially in Europe, numerous scientific panels, including the U.S. Food and Drug Administration, have concluded that consumption of GM foods is safe, even in cases involving GM foods with genetic material from very distantly related organisms. Indeed, foods containing GM ingredients do not require special labeling in the United States, although some groups have continued to lobby to change this ruling. By 2006, although the majority of GM crops were still grown in the Americas, GM plants tailored for production and consumption in other parts of the world were in field tests. For example, sweet potatoes intended for Africa were modified for resistance to sweet potato feathery mottle virus (SPFMV) by inserting into the sweet potato genome a gene encoding a viral coat protein from the strain of virus that causes SPFMV. The premise for this modification was based on earlier studies in other plants such as tobacco in which introduction of viral coat proteins rendered plants resistant to the virus.

The "golden rice" intended for Asia was genetically modified to produce almost 20 times the beta-carotene of previous varieties. Golden rice was created by modifying the rice genome to include a gene from the daffodil *Narcissus pseudonarcissus* that produces an enzyme known as phyotene synthase and a gene from the bacterium *Erwinia uredovora* that produces an enzyme called phyotene desaturase. The introduction of these genes enabled beta-carotene, which is converted to vitamin A in the human liver, to accumulate in the rice endosperm—the edible part of the rice plant—thereby increasing the amount of beta-carotene available for vitamin A synthesis in the body.

Another form of modified rice was generated to help combat iron deficiency, which impacts close to 30 percent of the world population. This GM crop was engineered by introducing into the rice genome a ferritin gene from the common bean *Phaseolus vulgaris* that produces a protein capable of binding iron, as well as a gene from the fungus *Aspergillus fumigatus* that produces an enzyme capable of digesting compounds that increase iron bioavailability via digestion of phytate (an inhibitor of iron absorption). The iron-fortified GM rice was engineered to overexpress an existing rice gene that produces a cysteine-rich metallothioneinlike (metal-binding) protein that enhances iron absorption.

A variety of other crops modified to endure the weather extremes common in other parts of the globe are also in production.

CHAPTER 6

PEOPLE'S RIGHT TO KNOW AND GMO PRODUCTION

W hen Rachel Carson's *Silent Spring* was published in 1962, many pesticides were being used freely and liberally despite the physical ailments they were causing in people. As mentioned in Chapter 4, Carson was attacked by the chemical industry as being an alarmist, an overzealous reformer, and someone doing more harm than good. Only after an investigation backed by President John F. Kennedy validated her findings did she become vindicated in her viewpoints.

Since the seminal work was published, dangerous pesticides like DDT have been banned in the United States. People are now open to questioning the scientific status quo and methods that may be dangerous. But it would be incorrect to say that scientific progress, consumers, and chemical companies have found a harmonious balance. Debates over genetically modified foods today are as heated as pesticide protests half a century earlier. Corporate lobbying has helped genetically modified foods become available to consumers while scientists are divided over their use.

A major debate point regarding GMOs is food labeling. Critics of GM foods argue that consumers

The supermarket chain Whole Foods now requires its suppliers to put GMO labels on any products that contain genetically modified ingredients. Some suppliers also include labels that trumpet their non-GMO status.

have a right to know what ingredients make up the food they purchase, then decide for themselves whether they want to eat it or not. Without proper labeling, consumers unknowingly ingest foods that they may not have otherwise purchased if they knew what ingredients were used. Many Americans are demanding to know what they are eating. However, food manufacturers contend that labeling genetically modified products would cause increases in food prices and unnecessary worry among the general public. A food company executive states that a label "implies the product is bad for you when there is no basis for that."

The food labeling movement has come to be known as the "right to know." The public response to genetically modified foods makes the issue a sensitive one for lawmakers and officials. Measures enforcing or striking down labeling laws are contentiously battled over. The issue is not just in the United States. In May 2013, activists turned out around the globe for anti-GM rallies. Just a month later, Monsanto dropped its bid to get more GM crops onto the European market, citing widespread opposition.

Because of their relative newness, GMOs have not been around long enough to determine their long-term health effects. The FDA says that they do not need to conduct safety reviews of whole foods derived from plants. Scientific studies have shown that GMOs do not pose a significant threat to consumers.

Critics claim it is impossible to know what effects genetically modified foods will manifest across multiple generations. Over time, further testing and exposure to people will ultimately show who is right. Some early testing on laboratory rats stirred up more controversy. In September 2012, French scientists from the University of Caen published a study showing that rats that were fed a diet containing NK603, a corn seed resistant to Monsanto's Roundup weed-killer, died earlier than rats fed a standard diet. While the European Food Safety Authority rejected the study, claiming its design, reporting, and analysis were inadequate, Russia banned the NK603 corn. In an effort to recreate the French study, Russian scientists set up a year-long experiment using web cameras installed in the rats' cages so that their progress could be monitored by anyone.

In the *New York Times Magazine* in 1998, Phil Angell, Director of corporate communications for Monsanto, stated that "Monsanto should not have to vouchsafe the safety of biotech food. Our interest is in selling as much of it as possible. Assuring its safety is the FDA's job."

EARLY DAYS OF GMOS

New hybrids of corn were introduced in the 1930s by Milford Beeghly. The new varieties of corn were more resistant to insects and were easier to grow. Many people, including some farmers, rejected the corn, claiming that it was "against nature." However, hybrid corn was a commercial success and now comprises most of the corn Americans eat. Hybridization, which is pollinating one species with the pollen from another species, is artificial cross-pollination. Some scientists consider it a crude form of genetic engineering.

By 2010, about 75 percent of processed food sold in the United States contained genetically modified ingredients. More than 50 percent of corn grown in the United States is from genetically modified seeds. GM soybeans in particular comprise 90 percent of the soybean production in the United States. Genetically modified crops claim over one hundred million acres of farmland in the United States, and the biotechnology industry includes over 1,000 companies totaling revenues close to $50 billion per year. Most present-day domesticated plants have been genetically altered so drastically that the new varieties cannot survive in the wild. Some plants are so different from their predecessors that they defy ancestral identification.

But it was not always so widespread. GMOs have been met with consumer and regulatory resistance in many countries owing to concerns over the potential unknown dangers to humans and the environment. When Stanley Cohen and Herbert Boyer released recombinant DNA into the world, many viewed it as simply an extension of historic agricultural practices only with more specific results. Governments had to step in to alleviate fears over unpredictable physiological or biochemical effects.

GMO REGULATORY POLICIES IN THE UNITED STATES

Biotechnology regulation in the United States began with a cautious approach. In 1974, scientists called for a temporary moratorium on genetic engineering. A conference of biologists concurred with this idea. By 1976, the National Institutes of Health (NIH) introduced guidelines for laboratories conducting experiments and research on recombinant DNA that were funded by the federal government. However, it was becoming clear that genetically modifying crops had the potential for incredible commercial success. Any regulations put forth by the government would come to be seen as a roadblock to financial gain. More research and experimentation was undertaken by companies in the private sector who were under no obligation to follow federal regulations. The guidelines and regulations made by the NIH were losing influence.

The United States federal government adopted a science-based interagency policy in 1986 called the Coordinated Framework for Regulation of Biotechnology, or Coordinated Framework. The Coordinated Framework established genetically modified food oversight responsibility among several departments: the US Department of Agriculture's Animal and Plant Health Inspection Service (USDA-APHIS), the Environmental Protection Agency (EPA), and the Department of Health and Human Services' Food and Drug Administration.

The three organizations share the responsibility of overseeing GMO use in the US. Generally speaking, the USDA-APHIS regulates the development and testing of most GMOs, while the EPA oversees the development and release of genetically modified plants with pest control properties. The FDA's responsibility lies with human food and animal feed safety.

The Federal Food, Drug, and Cosmetic Act (FDCA) gives the Food and Drug Administration power to ensure the safety and wholesomeness of all foods, excluding meat and poultry, in the United States. Under the FDCA the FDA is also charged with the safety of human and animal food including genetically modified foods. Genetically engineered foods and food ingredients must meet the same safety standards as conventional food products.

BIOTECHNOLOGY POLICY

Among the first food substances produced through biotechnology to come under FDA regulation was chymosin, in 1990. Chymosin is a milk clotting enzyme used in dairy products such as cheese. New food additives have to meet pre-market testing approval requirements. Chymosin, a recombinant DNA food ingredient was eventually found to be "generally recognized as safe" and was thus exempted from the new food additive requirements.

The food industry requested an explanation and clarification of the FDA's oversight framework, which led to the FDA publishing its "Statement of Policy: Foods Derived from New Plant Varieties" in May of 1992. The policy established the FDA's standard for assuring the safety and wholesomeness of conventional and bioengineered foods and animal feeds through explaining how these products are regulated. Further, it clarified the FDA's interpretation of human foods and animal feeds derived from new plant varieties specified in the FDCA, and gave guidance on scientific and regulatory issues regarding these foods.

LABELING

The FDA requires special labeling on food only if the composition of a bioengineered food is significantly different from the conventional version of the same food. The determination of significant difference is made by the FDA. The 1992 policy established that if a genetically engineered food is deemed indistinguishable from the traditionally bred equivalent by the FDA, then there are no special label requirements for disclosing the development method for the bioengineered food. In 1994, the FDA found that the Flavr Savr tomato was "as safe as tomatoes bred by conventional means." The manufacturer of this GM tomato, Calgene, made the decision to include special labeling on their product to alert consumers that the new tomato was developed through genetic engineering. However, they were not required to do so by the FDA. The FDA issued guidelines in 2001 for the voluntary labeling of genetically modified food for food manufacturers who wished to avoid misleading consumers. The purpose of the voluntary labeling guidelines is to give manufacturers the option to ensure truthfulness between themselves and their customers.

According to the FDA, labeling genetically modified foods is only mandatory in the event that the food itself poses potential safety problems for consumers. This policy still stands today.

The FDA and other scientific panels found that GMOs posed no threat in human consumption and the labeling rules reflected these findings. However, that has not deterred various groups from lobbying to have the labeling laws changed. These groups warn that human health is at risk with regards to genetically modified foods. As previously discussed, the addition of genes to create new proteins thereby creating transgenic foods can affect allergenic properties. They also cite the occurrences of

LABELING IN CANADA AND EUROPE

In Canada, the Canadian Food Inspection Agency (CFIA) and Health Canada both oversee food labeling under the Food and Drugs Act. Health Canada's mandate to protect public health and safety include ensuring there is proper labeling for food. Consumers are protected from fraudulent and misrepresentative food labeling, packaging, and advertising by the CFIA. Environment Canada, a Canadian department tasked with protecting the environment, is responsible for ensuring that no harmful substances are introduced into Canada.

Like in the United States, labeling is required only for GM foods that are significantly different from the conventionally grown varieties. Labeling is also required in scenarios where special labeling can mitigate potential dangers to human health. GM foods that have altered nutritional value or composition must be labeled to alert consumers, as do foods with allergens. Labeling for the sole purpose of indicating genetically engineered food is not required, but labels must state the nature of the nutritional change, compositional change, or presence of allergens. Similar to the United States voluntary labeling is an option for both GM and non-GM foods as long as the labels meet certain standards which avoid deception and are not purposefully misleading.

In Europe, authorized GMOs must satisfy the requirements spelled out by Regulation (EC) No. 1829/2003, which covers labeling, and Regulation (EC) No. 1830/2003, which covers labeling and traceability. Labels must specifically use the words "genetically modified," "contains

(*continued on the next page*)

(continued from the previous page)

genetically modified," or "produced from genetically modified" ingredients or organisms. Labels must also mention distinctive characteristics or physical properties when the food or feed raises ethical or religious concerns or differs from its conventional counterpart in composition, nutritional value, intended use, or health implications.

The European regulations specifically single out foods containing less than 1 percent of genetically modified material of the total food ingredients. In these cases, where GMOs may be "adventitious or technically unavoidable," the labeling is not required. However, earning this exception requires authorities to ensure that appropriate steps were taken to prevent the presence of GMOs.

insects that have evolved into insecticide-resistant "superbugs."

World governments do not agree on the potential dangers and risks that genetically modified foods pose. The European Union (EU) introduced strict labeling laws and a moratorium on the growth and import of genetically modified crops in 1998. This has led to precarious trade disputes between countries with more open GMO policies such as the United States, Canada, China, Argentina, and Australia and countries with stricter stances such as those in Europe and several African states. In Africa, international food aid that includes food or crops with GMO ingredients has been rejected. The difference between the opposing stance of the EU and the United States regarding GMOs seems to be one of semantics. The EU finds that there is not enough research to prove the safety of GMOs while the United States finds that there is not enough research to prove that they are unsafe.

CURRENT STATE OF GMOS

Today, genetically modified foods are a contentious subject among a variety of groups. Environmentalists, including environmental scientists, view GMOs as understudied, and a tool used by big businesses to control food production while suppressing local farmers in order to make a profit. Other opponents believe that the money spent on developing GMOs could be spent on organic farming instead. Because GMOs are still a new concept, legitimate concerns have been raised about long-term human and environmental effects. The FDA itself states, "Theoretically, genetic modifications have the potential to activate cryptic pathways synthesizing unknown or unexpected toxicants, or to increase expression from active pathways that ordinarily produce low or undetectable levels of toxicants." Critics believe that consumers should be protected from genetically modified ingredients and foods by adding warning labels on all applicable products.

GMO supporters, which include scientists and farmers, view the new varieties of crops as the key ingredient to solving the food shortages to come as

Whitley Marshall, president of Green Initiatives, speaks to protesters on World Food Day, October 12, 2013.

the world population explodes. Critics of GMOs are seen as alarmists, antiscience, and simply deniers of experimental truths. Supporters of GMOs cite numerous benefits as reasons to continue their production, which include visual perfection; resistance to viruses, fungi, and bacterial growth; ability to grow faster; resistance to pests thus reducing the need for potentially harmful pesticides; ability to tolerate extreme weather conditions such as cold fronts and droughts, and to grow in diverse geographical regions; and potential for producing added vitamins and nutrients which is vital in countries suffering from malnutrition.

Old political lines have been crossed when it comes to the GMO controversy. Historically, scientists and political liberals have sided with each other when it comes to major public debates. For example, the two groups agree on stem cell research, climate change, and evolution. However, political liberals and scientists are in opposition on the GMO issue while political conservatives (who have tended to oppose scientists on stem cells, climate change, and evolution) have aligned themselves with the scientific community with regard to GMOs.

In 1999, the United States saw an increase in public awareness of and opposition to genetically modified foods and seeds. The Bt corn controversy in 1999 made monarch butterflies the symbol of the environmental hazards presented by genetically modified crops. The butterflies were shown to be less populous in places where Bt corn was grown. Consumer organizations such as Public Citizen and the Sierra Club came out publicly against GMOs and questioned their safety. In 1999, a *Time* magazine poll reported that 81 percent of respondents were in favour of mandatory labels on genetically engineered foods.

GOVERNMENT RESPONSE

In November of 1999, following the first congressional hearing on GMOs, legislation was introduced in Congress that would require labeling of genetically modified foods. The FDA held hearings throughout the United States to determine whether more testing would be required to ensure consumer safety, and whether genetically modified foods should be considered an additive. If GMOs officially became an additive, the inclusion of them in processed foods would require mandatory labeling. Following the Bt corn controversy, the EPA asked companies that marketed corn that produces Bt toxin to have their farmers voluntarily plant a buffer zone of non-genetically modified corn to protect monarch butterflies. It was initially believed that the toxin produced by Bt corn did direct harm to the butterflies, however, it was the milkweed plants that the butterfly caterpillars lived on that were affected. An herbicide used with the corn reduced the milkweed plants in the area. The buffer-zone proposed by the EPA would allow the milkweed to grow and therefore leave the monarch butterfly population unaffected. The EPA also began investigating whether genetically modified seeds should be subject to pest control regulations.

Under President Bill Clinton's plan to increase funding for research into genetically engineered crops and their potential dangers, the FDA strengthened the

These plants can be harmed by an herbicide used with Bt corn, which affected the population of monarch butterflies.

bioengineered food review process and wrote guidelines for companies that wanted to label their GMO-free products. The Internet was just becoming a popular communication tool, so the FDA took advantage of this new technology. GMO producers were required to publish research and safety data on websites for consumers to read for themselves. Today, there are over 40 seeds and plants approved by the FDA for genetic modification all of which are available for public review via the websites of the companies that produce them.

RIGHT TO KNOW

The FDA's Statement of Policy says, "Section 402(a)(1) of the act imposes a legal duty on those who introduce food into the marketplace, including food derived from new crop varieties, to ensure that the food satisfies the applicable safety standard." This leaves it up to the companies themselves to ensure public safety regarding their genetically modified products, which seems in direct opposition to the statement given by a spokesperson for Monsanto.

There is a belief that consumers have a right to know what is in their food. The debate over food labeling is not necessarily about the safety of genetically modified foods, but rather what exactly is in the food supply. Consumers want to know how their food is grown. Opponents of labeling laws believe that they will harm growers and sellers of GMO crops and ingredients by inciting fear in customers when the research thus far does not support ill effects from GMOs. There will be economic implications resulting from these laws. Opponents say that the average family's food bill will increase by several hundred dollars per year, a number labeling supporters say is overstated.

Issues of free speech and commerce are also involved in the GMO debate. Labeling laws which would enable consumers' right to know could be at odds with the First Amendment and Commerce Clause which asserts that states do not have the ability to restrict commercial speech.

A beet farmer named Paul Schlagel whose beets are processed into granular sugar says that, "When you process the sugar beets, there's no GE material in the sugar. The sugar is identical to conventionally grown sugar, sugar cane, even organic sugar." He believes that laws that require labeling are a mistake. "It's just misinformation. It's misleading."

In Hawaii, papaya farmers' crops were saved after an outbreak of papaya ringspot virus in the mid-1990s. The virus would have decimated the crop, and bankrupted farmers, but the rainbow papaya, which was engineered with a gene from the virus itself that made the crop immune, saved the papaya crops and the farmers who were headed to financial ruin. The rainbow papaya also reduced the use of chemicals on the crops because the virus was spread by insects which growers tried to control

Hawaiian papaya trees like these were threatened by an outbreak of ringspot virus. Farmers embraced the GM Rainbow papaya, which saved their livelihoods.

with pesticides. As a ban on GMOs was proposed in Hawaii in early 2014, farmers whose livelihoods had been saved, found themselves at odds with those in favor of the ban.

Those who support the use of GMOs assert that since science has yet to find serious health risks due to genetically modified foods there is no reason for the government to intervene. University of Denver constitutional law professor Justin Marceau says, "When you're compelling a business to say something or a producer to say something, there has to be some governmental interest. There has to be a substantial government interest."

LABELING LAWS ON STATE BALLOTS

Since there are no federal laws requiring labeling of genetically modified foods, the states have taken it upon themselves to create laws requiring labels or explicitly allow companies to exclude labeling on their products. In 2014, two states in the United States, Oregon and Colorado, let voters decide if foods made with genetically modified ingredients should require labeling. The two states were the latest battlegrounds in the fight between critics of GMOs and the food companies and seed makers that use biotechnology in crops and foods. The vote drew the attention of big food producers and agribusiness companies which were against the labeling laws while consumer advocacy groups, organic food producers, and other similar groups wanted labeling.

Opponents of labeling in Oregon spent $20.5 million to fight the measure, and $16.7 million in Colorado. The costly campaigns helped energize GMO technology backers. Pro-labeling supporters only spent $8.2 million in Oregon and less than $1 million in Colorado according to state records. This pattern follows similar battles in California in 2012 and Washington in 2013. In the four contests, those on the side against labeling have spent about four times the amount the pro-labeling campaigns spent.

Despite the large disparity in their campaign funds, the vote in Oregon was notably close. The results showed that 50.5 percent of votes were against required labels on genetically modified foods, narrowly defeating the 49.5 percent of votes for mandatory labels. Colorado's labeling measure called Proposition 105 also failed to pass, with the voting results 66 percent against labeling and 34 percent for. California's Proposition 37 and Washington State's Initiative 522 would have required warning labels on domestically produced genetically modified foods and ingredients. Perhaps foreshadowing the Oregon and Colorado votes, both the California proposition and Washington State initiative were also defeated.

Vermont is the first state to require labeling for genetically modified foods. The law is set to go into effect in July 2016. As he signed the measure into law, Governor Peter Shumlin said, "Today, we are the first state in America that says simply, 'Vermonters have spoken loud and clear: We want to know what's in our food. We are pro-choice. We are pro-information.'" However, it is widely believed that the law will be met with legal challenges from the food industry, food manufacturers, the Grocery Manufacturers Association and other industry groups, many of whom will cite the First Amendment and Commerce Clause.

Observers predict that the GMO labeling debate will head to the national stage. Labeling supporters are hoping a federal mandate on genetically modified food labels will help consumers know what they are eating while opponents are hoping a law will nullify mandatory labeling laws. Executive director Scott Faber of Just Label It, a national advocacy organization, says that losses in Oregon and Colorado will not abate consumers' right to know what their food contains. "The fight will shift to the nation's capitol," Faber said.

Jim Greenwood, chief executive officer of the Biotechnology Industry Organization, said in a statement, "The GMO labeling discussion deserves a national solution. We will continue to explore policies that provide consumers with information about the foods we eat."

CORPORATE RESPONSE

Fighting against the potential labeling laws in Oregon and Colorado were large corporations such as Kraft Foods Group Inc., PepsiCo Inc., and Monsanto Company. The food industry is also supporting any legislation that would strike down any requirements for mandatory labeling of genetically modified foods and crops. For example, U.S. House Representative Mike Pompeo of Kansas introduced a bill in 2014 that would bar individual states from requiring GMO labeling. As of December 2014, that bill had yet to pass into law, and has direct competition in the form of an act called the Genetically Engineered Food Right-to-Know Act, which creates a mandatory federal labeling law.

The percentage of farmlands dedicated to GMOs has risen over the years, and staples such as corn and cotton have more GMO variations than not. Consumers have been using GM food at a steadily increasing rate, however, many companies continue to put a lot of money into backing antilabeling legislation. Other companies are choosing to enable consumers' right-to-know. Many U.S. companies such as Frito-Lay, McDonalds, Gerber, and McCain Foods publicly announced that they would not purchase foods made with genetically altered seeds.

MONSANTO COMPANY VS. FARMERS

In 1980, the United States Supreme Court set a new precedent allowing seeds to be patented. The Monsanto Company took full advantage of the ruling and set out to patent its genetically modified seeds. Since then, Monsanto has taken control of the genetic seed industry and owned 674 biotechnology patents as of 2008. According to U.S. Department of Agriculture data, Monsanto has won more patents than any other company. Not only do they produce one of the most widely used weed killers or herbicides called Roundup, but they also produce seeds that are resistant to Roundup.

The company faces many allegations from consumer groups and farmers—many of the same groups Monsanto goes after for patent violations. Court documents show that Monsanto sends agents into communities to secretly gather surveillance evidence of possible patent infringement. Farmers have come to call these investigators the "seed police." Farmers who use Monsanto seeds must sign a contract which includes the stipulation that they will not collect and reuse seeds in subsequent crops, forcing farmers to abandon a centuries-old practice of saving seeds after a harvest. It also forces farmers to buy new seeds every planting season. Monsanto defends their policies as its way of protecting its patents and stopping those who "reap the benefits of the technology without paying for its use." Monsanto spokesman Darren Wallis told the magazine *Vanity Fair* that Monsanto "spends more than $2 million a day in research to identify, test, develop and bring to market innovative new seeds and technologies that benefit farmers."

The company, as they did in Colorado and Oregon, fights labeling measures. In Maui, voters narrowly passed a measure in 2014 that bans growing genetically modified crops until after an analysis of its health impact is reviewed by the county. Monsanto plans to legally challenge this measure. A spokeswoman says that it would have major negative effects on the local economy, Hawaiian agriculture, and Monsanto's business on the island.

In addition to supporting antilabeling campaigns, Monsanto has backed a group called American Farmers for the Advancement and Conservation of Technology (AFACT). The group led efforts to fight pro-labeling groups, and hoped to discredit "questionable labeling tactics and activism" by marketers leading consumers away from foods that make use of new technology.

SUPERMARKETS AND CHEFS

In 2013, the FDA considered approving the genetically engineered salmon AquAdvantage for sale in the United States A number of major grocery chains including Trader Joes, Aldi, Whole Foods Market, Kroger, and others oppose the sale of this fish.

Engineered by the company AquaBounty, one of the AquAdvantage salmon's added genes keeps a growth hormone activated after it would normally be shut down. The faster growing salmon would make farming salmon in the United States a viable option as opposed to importing salmon from abroad as it is today. As of December 2014, the FDA has yet to make an official decision on the salmon.

In addition to refusing to sell genetically modified salmon, Whole Foods Market is requiring suppliers to label products with GMO ingredients. Their concern is the inability of its customers to choose to purchase non-GMO products. Labeling, they argue, will allow consumers to make informed purchases. The company reports that their Non-GMO™ Project products are "among the fastest growing sellers in our non-perishable grocery category."

Chefs are following suit. Tom Colicchio, founder of Craft restaurants and judge on the TV show "Top Chef," is one of the chefs delivering a petition signed by over 700 culinary professionals demanding GMO labeling to lawmakers in Washington, D.C. The petition came at the same time that the House Agriculture Committee looked over the bill introduced by Kansas congressman, Rep. Mike Pompeo. Colicchio and other chefs are reducing or completely removing genetically modified ingredients from their kitchens.

Chef Tom Colicchio testifies before Congress in 2010 about improving nutrition. He later joined a group calling on Congress to support labeling of GMOs.

SCIENTIFIC VIEWPOINT

Many lawmakers do not see genetically modified foods as a potential hazard to the public. British Parliament member George Freeman defended GMOs when he told farmers, "The resilience we need for the future will be delivered by smart plant breeding–and that's all GM is." Billionaire and Microsoft founder Bill Gates believes in biotechnology's ability to solve world hunger problems. "By spending a relatively little amount of money on proven solutions, we can help poor farmers feed themselves," he said in a letter in January 2012. For the most part, scientists agree.

The National Academy of Sciences endorsed the safety of biotech foods in May 2000. The panel stated that inserting genes from one species into another was not inherently dangerous. However, they recommended a long-term study to determine the effects of genetically modified foods over time. They also recommended that the EPA strengthen its oversight of all GMOs including those excluded from their rules from 1994.

In 2010, the National Academy of Sciences released another report titled, "Impact of Genetically Engineered Crops on Farm Sustainability in the United States." The report established that the global scientific consensus was that not only are genetically modified crops providing observable benefits, but they are also no riskier than others. The paper stated, "In general, the committee finds that genetic-engineering technology has produced substantial net environmental and economic benefits to U.S. farmers compared with non-GE crops in conventional agriculture."

The American Association for the Advancement of Science and the World Health Organization support scientific findings that have yet to find adverse effects caused by eating GM foods and crops. Many scientists say labeling initiatives are fueled not by science but by misconceptions about GMO technology.

Biotech companies maintain that genetically modified crops are thoroughly tested with in-depth analyses designed to meet federal safety standards. Scientists discontinued splicing a Brazilian nut gene into soybeans when research showed it might sicken people with nut allergies.

Yet questions remain. Although scientific research has led many to believe that GMOs do not pose a threat to people, other research in the agricultural field has hindered public opinion toward the credibility of scientific research. In 2013, a paper tying cancer in rats to genetically modified food had to be retracted.

MODIFIED CORN AND CANCER

In 2012, the food safety journal *Food and Chemical Toxicology* published a paper that linked genetically modified corn and Monsanto's Roundup to cancer and premature death in rats. The main author, Gilles-Eric Séralini of the University of Caen in France, had previously undertaken other studies challenging the safety of GMOs. This particular study followed 200 rats for two years. Different groups of rats were fed different amounts of a Monsanto genetically engineered corn made to be resistant to Roundup and water mixed with the herbicide. Results showed that the rats fed GM corn had higher incidence of tumors and early death than the control group that was fed non-modified corn and plain water.

However after passing the peer review process, there were numerous critics of the study. Many scientists accused the study of being flawed, sensationalistic, and possibly fraudulent. Concerns over the study included the number of rats being too small, the rat breed being naturally prone to cancer, and that the results were inconclusive. Food labeling supporters touted the study as did opponents of biotech foods. In the end, the journal's editor A. Wallace Hayes retracted the paper. Hayes said that the study's results were not incorrect or fraudulent, but they were also "inconclusive, and therefore do not reach the threshold of publication."

Scientists from the Russian agency National Association for Genetic Safety endeavored to recreate the University of Caen study and broadcast it live over the internet. According to their website, as of 2013, they were still working to launch a fundraising campaign to conduct the study.

CONCERNS FROM VARIOUS FIELDS

While agricultural scientists and biotechnologists may generally agree on the safety of genetically modified foods, professionals in other fields of study are not as supportive. Some in the medical industry believe that GMOs could introduce new allergens to the public. Others believe that the antibiotic resistance of GMOs could transfer to the bacteria in the human digestive system thus making it more difficult to get rid of certain bacteria once a person is infected.

Pediatric neurologist Dr. Martha R. Herbert takes issue with supermarkets making GMOs available to the public without proper labeling. She sees the practice as an experiment conducted without participants' consent, and she asserts that it is both illegal and unethical. In an article published on the Organic Consumers Association website, Herbert writes, "Although scientists are well aware that genetic engineering can produce unexpected, often highly undesirable effects, there is no current testing or health monitoring to detect these health and environmental curve-balls." She goes on to describe a genetically altered form of tryptophan which was sold in 1989 and was responsible for thousands of illnesses, 1500 cases of permanent disability, and 37 deaths.

There are calls for more testing before making GMOs widely available. In 2001, Dr. Margaret Mellon, director of the agricultural and biotechnology program, Union of Concerned Scientists, considered the number of studies looking into the safety of genetically engineered foods as inadequate. Mellon also asserts that the argument by some scientists that GMOs are a minor extension of traditional breeding, is not enough.

Some scientists believe that consumers should know what goes into their food and into their bodies. If someone becomes ill due to a genetically modified ingredient, without proper labeling it would be impossible to trace the source of the illness. In a *New York Times* article published in December 2000, Dr. Michael Jacobson, director of the Center for Science in the Public Interest, supported more regulations for GMOs. "Now is the time, while agricultural biotechnology is still young, for Congress and regulatory agencies to create the framework that will maximize the safe use of these products, bolster public confidence in them, and allow all of humankind to benefit from their enormous potential."

CONCLUSION

While GMOs offer many potential benefits to society, the potential risks associated with them have fueled controversy, especially in the food industry. Many skeptics warn about the dangers that GM crops may pose to human health. For example, genetic manipulation may potentially alter the allergenic properties of crops. However, the more-established risk involves the potential spread of engineered crop genes to native flora and the possible evolution of insecticide-resistant superweeds and superbugs, and the issues of reduced bee and butterfly populations. In 1998 the EU addressed such concerns by implementing strict GMO labeling laws and a moratorium on the growth and import of GM crops. In addition, the stance of the EU on GM crops has led to trade disputes with the United States, which, by comparison, has accepted GM foods very openly. The FDA has given approval to GMOs, but they acknowledge the controversy that still surrounds their use. Other countries, such as Canada, China, Argentina, and Australia, also have open policies on GM foods, but some African states have rejected international food aid containing GM crops.

The resurgence of organic farming using techniques that have been used for centuries produces more biodiverse crops, something that is not achieved through genetic manipulation, where the crops are all engineered to have little diversity. The Irish Potato Famine was a result of a lack of diversity in the crop, and with newly generated superweeds and superbugs due to GM crops, an attack that could lead to crop decimation is another concern that could affect both the health of consumers as well as the financial health of agribusiness.

One of the arguments for the continued development of GM crops and food is its potential to eliminate food insecurity. However, a report titled "Feeding the World Without GMOs" released in April 2015 debunks that claim, indicating that traditional methods are "shown to actually increase food supplies and reduce the environmental impact of production." The report by the Environmental Working Group was funded by the Just Label It campaign.

Many of the questions regarding the health and safety of genetically modified crops and food can only be solved over time. Until then, it will be difficult to assess the veracity of arguments for either side regarding long-term effects. However scientists agree that testing should be conducted and careful oversight given to this new technology. New research results are published every year while new genetically engineered foods are being created by biotechnology companies like Monsanto Corporation.

As in Shelley's classic tale, Dr. Frankenstein, his creation, and the frightened villagers would probably have all benefitted by first taking the time to properly assess the true nature of the beast.

ALLELE Any of the alternative forms of a gene that may occur at a given locus.

COVER CROP A crop planted to prevent soil erosion and to provide humus.

CULTIGENS A cultivated or domestic organism which has diverged enough while in domestication or cultivation from its ancestors or closest wild relatives to be classified as a species, subspecies, or major variety.

DOMESTICATE To raise an animal or grow a plant for human use.

DOMINANT Exerting ecological or genetic prominence.

DRYLAND FARMING Practicing agricultural methods suited to arid regions.

ENTOMOLOGISTS Scientists who study insects.

EXTRACHROMOSOMAL Situated or controlled by factors outside the chromosome.

FERTILITY The ability to produce young; the ability to support the growth of many plants.

FUSION A process in which the nuclei of atoms are joined.

GENOME One haploid set of chromosomes with the genes they contain; the genetic material of an organism.

HETEROZYGOUS Having the two alleles at corresponding loci on homologous chromosomes different for one or more loci.

HOMOZYGOUS Having the two genes at corresponding loci on homologous chromosomes identical for one or more loci.

HORMONES Natural substances produced in the body that influence the way the body grows or develops.

HYBRID An animal or plant that is produced from two animals or plants of different kinds.

HYDROLOGISTS Scientists who deal with the properties, distribution, and circulation of water on and below Earth's surface and in the atmosphere.

IRRADIATION Exposure to radiation.

IRRIGATION The watering of land by artificial means to foster plant growth.

LAW OF INDEPENDENT ASSORTMENT A principle in genetics limited and modified by the subsequent discovery of the phenomenon of linkage: the different pairs of hereditary units are distributed to the gametes independently of each other, the gametes combine at random, and the various combinations of hereditary pairs occur in the zygotes according to the laws of chance.

LAW OF SEGREGATION A principle in genetics in which hereditary units occur in pairs that separate during gamete formation so that every gamete receives but one member of a pair.

MUTAGENESIS The occurrence or induction of mutation.

OUTBREEDING The interbreeding of stock that are relatively unrelated.

PHENOTYPES Observable properties of an organism that are produced by the interaction of the genotype and the environment.

PLANTPATHOLOGISTS Specialists concerned with the diseases of plants.

PLASMID DNA, found especially in bacteria, that is physically separate from, and can replicate independently of, the bacterium's chromosomal DNA.

PROPAGATION Increasing an organism in numbers.

QUIESCENT Being in a state of arrest.

RECESSIVE Expressed only when the determining gene is in the homozygous condition.

RECOMBINANT DNA Genetically engineered DNA usually incorporating DNA from more than one species of organism.

TRANSGENIC Being or used to produce an organism or cell of one species into which one or more genes of other species have been incorporated.

TRIPLOID Having or being a chromosome number three times the monoploid number.

VETCH A plant that has small flowers and is used to feed farm animals.

AGRICULTURE

Articles from new research in agriculture and the effects of genetic modification on the agricultural industry are included in the following listings. John Becklake and Sue Becklake, *Food and Farming* (1991). Boy Scouts of America, *Agribusiness* (1987). Gordon Conway and E.B Barbier, *After the Green Revolution* (1990). Daniel Charles, *Lords of the Harvest* (2001). J.F Hart, *Land That Feeds Us* (Norton, 1991). Mark Lambert, *Farming and the Environment* (Steck, 1990). NPR, "Farm Dinners Serve Up Local Food, Ambiance" (2011). *Food & Wine*, "Grow for Good" (2014). EPA, "Organic Farming." Nature, "A growing problem" (2014). The National Academies Press, *Impact of Genetically Engineered Crops on Farm Sustainability in the United States* (2010). Becca Aaronson, "Championing the Farm to Table Food Movement" (2012). Donald L. Barlett, and James B. Steele. "Monsanto's Harvest of Fear" (2008). David Biello, "Will Organic Food Fail to Feed the World?" (2012). Chris Hastings, "Chefs with Issues: Farm-to-table Should Still Be on the Table" (2013). Justin Kastner, *Food and Agriculture Security an Historical, Multidisciplinary Approach* (2011). Anna Lappe, "Yes, Organic Farming Can Feed the World" (2014). John Metcalfe, "One of America's Most Famous Slow-Food Chefs Says Farm-to-Table 'Doesn't Really Work'" (2014). Nick Meyer, "UN Report Says Small-

Scale Organic Farming Only Way to Feed the World"
(2013). Sakiko Parr, *The Gene Revolution GM Crops and
Unequal Development* (2007). Richard Schiffman, "An
Insurance Policy for Climate Change? How Seed
Banks Are Protecting the Future of Food" (2014).
Ian Schwartz, "Sacramento Considering Allowing
Urban Farming To Fight Blight, Promote Farm-To-
Fork" (2014). Peter Tyson, "Should We Grow GM
Crops?" (2001).

AGRICULTURE IN ANCIENT ASIA

Hiuen Tsiang, *Si-yu-ki: Buddhist Records of the Western
World*, 2 vol., trans. by Samuel Beal (1884, reprinted
1981), offers travel accounts of early Chinese
Buddhist pilgrims to India in the 1st millennium,
including those of Shi Fahian, Song Yun, and Hiuen
Tsiang; Mabel Ping-Hua Lee, *The Economic History of
China* (1921, reprinted 1969), is a history of Chinese
agriculture with emphasis on soil depletion; Kwang-
Chih Chang, *The Archaeology of Ancient China*, 4th rev.
ed. (1986), is a modern text interpreting prehistoric
and protohistoric archaeological evidence in the
historical framework of cultural development
until 221 BCE (illustrated, with bibliography);
Ping-Ti-Ho, *Studies on the Population of China*, 1368–
1953 (1959, reprinted 1967), is a scholarly study of
population growth and of interacting variables,
such as migrations, land utilization and tenure,

and food-production techniques, with extensive data tables, bibliography, and notes; N.I. Vavilov, *The Origin, Variation, Immunity, and Breeding of Cultivated Plants* (1951), presents selected writings of one of the world's outstanding contributors to the theory of genetics, plant breeding, and study of plant variation, systematics, and evolution (illustrated, with selected bibliography); J.W. McCrindle, *McCrindle's Ancient India: As Described by Megasthenes and Arrian* (1877, reissued 1984); Ifran Habib, *The Agrarian System of Mughal India* (1556–1707) (1963), is an informative text that covers cultivation techniques, crops, land tenure, village communities, and revenue administration; and Andrew M. Watson, *Agricultural Innovation in the Early Islamic World* (1983), is a systematic, informative overview.

AGRICULTURE IN EUROPE FROM 200 BCE TO 1600 CE

G.E. Fussell, *Farming Technique from Prehistoric to Modern Times* (1966), is a general review of the history of agricultural tools and techniques, with many illustrations and an extensive bibliography; David Grigg, *The Dynamics of Agricultural Change* (1982), is a survey of historical sources. Jean Philippe Lévy, *The Economic Life of the Ancient World* (1967;

originally published in French, 1964), describes the various economies of the Greco-Oriental world in the time before Alexander, during the Hellenistic Age, in the early Roman Empire, and also in the later Roman Empire; Fritz M. Heichelheim, *An Ancient Economic History*, rev. ed., 3 vol. (1958–70; originally published in German, 1938), contains extensive and detailed information on ancient agriculture; see also standard editions of such Classical authors as Cato, Columella, Hesiod, Pliny, Varro, and Xenophon. Georges Duby, *Rural Economy and Country Life in the Medieval West* (1968, reprinted 1976; originally published in French, 1962), is a classic work on agriculture from the 9th to the 15th century. Also useful are Robert Latouche, *The Birth of Western Economy*, 2nd ed. (1967, reprinted 1981; originally published in French, 1956); Lynn White, Jr., *Medieval Technology and Social Change* (1962, reissued 1980); B.H. Slicher Van Bath, *The Agrarian History of Western Europe*, AD 500–1850 (1963; originally published in Dutch, 1960); and Marc Bloch, *French Rural History* (1966; originally published in French, 1952–56). Broader surveys include Jerome Blum (ed.), *Our Forgotten Past: Seven Centuries of Life on the Land* (1982), a well-illustrated collection of essays; and Emmanuel Le Roy Ladurie and Joseph Goy, *Tithe and Agrarian History from the Fourteenth to the Nineteenth Centuries*, trans. from the French (1982), a comparative description of agricultural production in several countries.

ANIMAL BREEDING

Four good introductions to animal breeding are D.S. Falconer and Trudy F.C. Mackay, *Introduction to Quantitative Genetics*, 4th ed. (1996); Richard M. Bourdon, *Understanding Animal Breeding*, 2nd ed. (2000); R.A. Mrode and R. Thompson, *Linear Models for the Prediction of Animal Breeding Values*, 2nd ed. (2005); and Wilson G. Pond and Alan W. Bell (eds.), *Encyclopedia of Animal Science* (2005).

GENETICALLY MODIFIED ORGANISMS

Nigel G. Halford, *Genetically Modified Crops* (2003), gives a historical account of genetic technology in the food industry, discusses the safety of contemporary GM foods, and comments on the future of GM crops. Alan McHughen, *Pandora's Picnic Basket: The Potential and Hazards of Genetically Modified Foods* (2000), provides a skeptical perspective on the safety of GM foods, focusing on the policies related to production and distribution of GM foods. John E.J. Rasko, Gabrielle O'Sullivan, and Rachel A. Ankeny, *The Ethics of Inheritable Genetic Modification: A Dividing Line?* (2006), explores the application of gene technology to human medicine and the ethical implications of human genetic modification. John C. Avise, *The Hope, Hype, and Reality of Genetic Engineering: Remarkable Stories from Agriculture, Industry, Medicine, and the Environment* (2004), covers a broad range of topics, from agriculture to medicine to bioterrorism, in remarkable detail and with reasonable objectivity. The following articles discuss genetically modified crops and the fight for food labeling as well as actions that both companies and states are taking in the fight for and against GMOs. Worldwatch Institute, "Genetically Modified Crops Only a Fraction of Primary Global Crop Production" (2014). Kashi. com, "Kashi and the non-GMO Project". Jeff Akst. "Designer Livestock" (2014). Shicana Allen, "Fish Frenzy: GM Salmon Breed with Trout, Threaten Wild Populations" (2013). American Veterinary Medical Association, "Welfare Implications of Dehorning and Disbudding Cattle" (2014). Lisa Baertlein, "Genetically Modified Seafood: Whole Foods, Trader Joe's And Others Vow Not To Sell GMO Fish" (2013). David P Clark, and Nanette Jean Pazdernik. *Biotechnology: Applying the Genetic Revolution*. Academic Press/Elsevier. (2009). Lana J. Ellis, "Food Safety or Food Fight: Administrative Impact on Trade Policies Relating to Genetically Modified Organisms." (2010). Food Standards Agency, "Cloned animals" (2012). David H.

Freedman, "The Truth about Genetically Modified Food." (2013). Annie Gasparro, and Jacob Bunge, "Food Industry Wins Round in GMO-Labeling Fight" (2014). Carey Gillam, "GMO Labeling Fails in Colorado, Oregon; GMO Ban Passes in Maui" (2014). Terri Hallenbeck, "Vermont Gov Signs Law to Require Labels on GMO Foods." (2014). Terri Hallenbeck, "Ben and Jerry's says goodbye to GMOs" (2014). Amy Harmon, "A Lonely Quest for Facts on Genetically Modified Crops" (2014). Rachel Hennessey, "GMO Food Debate In The National Spotlight" (2012). Martha R Herbert, "Genetically Modified Food: Unsafe Until Further Notice" (2001). Ethan A Huff, "Tell the FDA 'NO!' to GMO fish." Jolie Lee, "What You Need to Know about GMOs." (2014). Jane Lindholm, "Some Food Companies Are Quietly Dumping GMO Ingredients" (2014). Diahanna Lynch, and David Vogel. "The Regulation of GMOs in Europe and the United States: A Case-Study of Contemporary European Regulatory Politics" (2001). Emily Main, "Target Launches New Organic GMO-Free Food Brand" (2013). Andrew Martin, "Is a Food Revolution Now in Season?" (2009). John H Perkins, *Geopolitics and the Green Revolution: Wheat, Genes, and the Cold War* (1997). Andrew Pollack, "Paper Tying Rat Cancer to Herbicide Is Retracted" (2013). Luke Runyon, "No Matter How Colorado Votes,

GMO Labeling Debate Far from over" (2014). Sarah Schmidt, "Genetically engineered pigs killed after funding ends" (2012). Tennille Tracy, "Chefs Push Lawmakers on Labeling Genetically Modified Food" (2014). University of California – Davis, "Goats' milk with antimicrobial lysozome speeds recovery from diarrhea" (2013). Bryan Walsh, "Foodies Can Eclipse (and Save) the Green Movement" (2011). Bryan Walsh, "Modifying the Endless Debate Over Genetically Modified Crops" (2013). Christie Wilcox, "Mythbusting 101: Organic Farming Conventional Agriculture | Science Sushi, Scientific American Blog Network" (2011).

GREGOR MENDEL

Hugo Iltis, *Life of Mendel* (1932, reissued 1966), is a classic biography, being a translation from the German of the major part of the author's *Gregor Johann Mendel: Leben, Werk und Wirkung* (1924). Robin Marantz Henig, *The Monk in the Garden: The Lost and Found Genius of Gregor Mendel, the Father of Genetics* (2000), is a highly readable and imaginative account of Mendel. Franz Weiling, "Historical Study: Johann Gregor Mendel 1822–1884," *American Journal of Medical Genetics*, 40(26):1–25 (July 1, 1991), is the most authoritative and informative essay about Mendel and is generously illustrated.

ORIGINS OF AGRICULTURE

A.B. Gebauer and T.D. Price (eds.), *Transitions to Agriculture in Prehistory* (1992); and T.D. Price and A.B. Gebauer (eds.), *Last Hunters, First Farmers: New Perspectives on the Prehistoric Transition to Agriculture* (1995), are overviews of events leading to agriculture around the world. B.D. Smith, *The Emergence of Agriculture* (1995), is an integrated overview of research methods, theoretical considerations, and archaeological sites pertinent to the development of agriculture. M. Woods and M.B. Woods, *Ancient Agriculture: From Foraging to Farming* (2000), discusses agricultural technology in various cultures from the Stone Age to 476 CE, including China, Egypt, Mesoamerica, and Greece. David Rindos, *The Origins of Agriculture: An Evolutionary Perspective* (1984), concentrates on agriculture as a natural biological process not unique to people; J. Desmond Clark and Steven A. Brandt (eds.), *From Hunters to Farmers: The Causes and Consequences of Food Production in Africa* (1984), analyzes economic changes in prehistoric society; T.D. Price, *Europe's First Farmers* (2000), gives an account of the development of farming in Europe. D.R. Piperno and D.M. Pearsall, *The Origins of Agriculture in the Lowland Neotropics* (1998), is the first assessment of the history and significance of tropical lowland agriculture in the Americas. Two excellent volumes that consider the designation of a fourth agricultural regime in North America are Douglas Deur and Nancy J. Turner (eds.), *Keeping it Living: Traditions of Plant Use and Cultivation on the Northwest Coast of North America* (2005); and Kat Anderson, *Tending the Wild: Native American Knowledge and the Management of California's Natural Resources* (2005).

PLANT DISEASE

General works include G.C. Ainsworth, *Introduction to the History of Plant Pathology* (1981), a review of the developments in the field of plant pathology and the influence of plant diseases on history; Gail L. Schumann, *Plant Diseases: Their Biology and Social Impact* (1991), a discussion of the social and cultural influence of plant diseases; and E.C. Large, *The Advance of the Fungi* (1940, reissued 1962), a popular account of plant disease epidemics and how they have influenced economic and political history.

RACHEL CARSON

Martha Freeman (ed.), *Always, Rachel* (1995), collects Carson's correspondence with her friend Dorothy Freeman during 1952–64. Carson's life and work are examined in Paul Brooks, *The House of Life: Rachel Carson at Work* (1972, reissued 1989), with selections from her published and unpublished material; H. Patricia Hynes, *The Recurring Silent Spring* (1989); Mary A. McCay, *Rachel Carson* (1993); Linda J. Lear, *Rachel Carson: Witness for Nature* (1997); and Arlene Rodda Quaratiello, *Rachel Carson: A Biography* (2004, reissued 2010).

Gardening
Horticulture